DIPLOMA

International Schools and University Entrance

DIPLOMA

International Schools
and University Entrance

by Martin Mayer

The Twentieth Century Fund
New York 1968

THE TWENTIETH CENTURY FUND founded in 1919 and endowed by Edward A. Filene, is a nonprofit foundation which, through research and publication, seeks to shed light on significant issues. Major fields of interest of the Fund are economics, social problems and international affairs. The study of which this volume is a report has been defined and supported by the Fund's Board of Trustees. The Fund attempts to ensure the scholarly quality of works appearing under its imprint; the Trustees and the staff, however, accord the author or authors complete freedom in the statement of opinions and the interpretation of facts.

BOARD OF TRUSTEES

Morris B. Abram
Adolf A. Berle
 Chairman
Francis Biddle
Jonathan B. Bingham
Arthur F. Burns
Erwin D. Canham
Evans Clark

Benjamin V. Cohen
J. Kenneth Galbraith
August Heckscher
David E. Lilienthal
Georges-Henri Martin
Lawrence K. Miller
Luis Muñoz-Marín

Don K. Price
James Rowe
 Vice Chairman
Arthur Schlesinger, Jr.
H. Chr. Sonne
 Treasurer
Herman W. Steinkraus
Charles P. Taft

Director: M. J. Rossant

Copyright © 1968 by the Twentieth Century Fund, Inc.
Printed in the United States of America
By Connecticut Printers, Incorporated, Hartford, Connecticut
Library of Congress Catalog Card Number: 68-26129

FOREWORD

Mr. Martin Mayer's book records one step in progress towards solution of a real human need.

Many thousands of families live outside their own countries on international missions. Their children must go to school in the countries where the families are stationed. United Nations servants, diplomats, businessmen, economic aid workers are faced with a difficult problem, for the secondary schools in which their children must study are not accredited in the universities of their own countries. No real reason exists why young people educated at a French lycée, a Swiss school, a German *Gymnasium*, a good preparatory or high school in the United States, or like institutions in Britain, the Netherlands or Italy, should be barred by universities in their own or (for that matter) in other countries for lack of adequate preparatory education. The Twentieth Century Fund therefore investigated the possibility of developing an "international baccalaureate"—a system of study and accreditation acceptable as widely as possible throughout the western world, beginning for experimental purposes with the non-public international schools. Mr. Mayer was asked to explore and report on the potentialities. This book is the account of what he found.

The specific proposal for an "international baccalaureate" is an invitation to pilot schools and universities to join in a great experiment the essence of which is to admit, in the years 1970–1976, candidates who will have received a secondary education accredited both as to content and quality of work by the resulting diploma. Organization of the experiment must be so arranged that it shall not be an easy way of evading established national examinations. By 1976 a balance sheet can be drawn, assessing the performance of students thus accredited.

Though this report is a chronicle of difficulties, it must not be considered discouraging. Paralleling Mr. Mayer's exploration, work was carried on with school and university authorities in Switzerland, France, Great Britain and is now beginning in the United States. Already several universities of the first rank have agreed to cooperate.

Let me add that this exploration—solving the human problem of children of families working abroad—may perhaps break the logjam. Access to university training, education and learning ought to be international and not national. Education consequently ought not to be chopped into nationalist compartments. Some sort of Nansen passport ought to emerge whereby youths can be trained anywhere in the western world and perhaps some day in the eastern world as well for access to universities everywhere else. At the moment this is a distant dream—but the search for an international baccalaureate may prove the initial breach in an artificial barrier presently disfiguring education. That the difficulties as well as the possibilities may be appreciated, Mr. Mayer's book is here presented. Meanwhile the Fund goes forward with the organizing work that, it is hoped, will resolve the underlying questions.

We are indebted not only to Mr. Mayer but to Georges-Henri Martin and to August Heckscher (Fund Trustees) and to many others for joining in the project. It is a tiny segment of the vast work for world order.

Adolf A. Berle
Chairman, Board of Trustees
The Twentieth Century Fund

41 East 70 Street, New York City, March 1968

CONTENTS

	Introduction	3
PART ONE	**The Problem**	
CHAPTER 1	The Education of Foreigners	17
CHAPTER 2	Access to Universities	37
PART TWO	**The Schools**	
CHAPTER 3	Ecolint, UNIS, and Atlantic College: The Sponsors of the Examination	69
CHAPTER 4	The Scholae Europaeae	97
CHAPTER 5	A Multinational Multitude	111
CHAPTER 6	The French Foreign Lycées	133
CHAPTER 7	American Overseas Schools	153
PART THREE	**The International Examination**	
CHAPTER 8	The Prospects for a Passport	183
CHAPTER 9	The International Baccalaureate Office	215
	Conclusion	235
	Index	241

INTRODUCTION

This book, like many another, had a rather odd origin. The man most responsible for starting it was Georges-Henri Martin, editor of *La Tribune de Genève*, formerly a foreign correspondent in Washington for French and Swiss papers. Both as a Genevese and as a journalist, M. Martin felt special concern for international relations of a technical and practical sort; and as the father of two boys at the International School of Geneva he was interested in the school's problems and future. Among the problems besetting the school was that of the different national certificates which students completing their secondary education at "Ecolint" would have to acquire if they hoped to be admitted to the universities of their home countries. Among the futures envisioned by the staff at the school was one in which an international university entrance examination — an International Baccalaureate — would replace national examinations as the seal of approval for the work done by the multinational student bodies of such schools.

In the autumn of 1964, M. Martin, as a trustee of the Twentieth Century Fund, arranged for August Heckscher, then director of the Fund, to meet with a committee of the Geneva school and discuss the question of an International Baccalaureate. Presently the Geneva school submitted to Mr. Heckscher the sketchy suggestions for an international examination which had been developed by its teachers, plus the minutes of two meetings of visiting educators at which the problem and the suggestions had been discussed in a preliminary way. Mr. Heckscher and I had met behind the many columns of the Executive Office Building in Washington, where he was President Kennedy's adviser on the arts and I was a participant in a study group called the Panel on Educational Research and Development. He sent the documents along to me with a query as to whether I might be interested in working on this problem.

Most of the documents were in both English and French. Browsing through them, I found that in literature and history the proposals in one language were simply translations of those in the other. But in mathematics, I found to my naïve surprise that the suggested programs were substantially different in emphasis and in content. After thinking a while about the reasons why agreement on syllabus should be more difficult in the supposedly neutral subject of mathematics, I told Mr. Heckscher that I was indeed interested in working on this problem, and we agreed that I should go to Geneva for a few days to form some opinion of the people who were trying to create a single secondary program for students from many countries, and of their chances for success.

On my return, I reported to Mr. Heckscher that the venture was in truth interesting — even fascinating — but that its organization was very weak. It would certainly not be possible for the group in Geneva to make noticeable progress toward

Introduction 5

their goal without a considerable investment of money. Mr. Heckscher felt that the Twentieth Century Fund could give the Geneva group only initial financial support, linked to a research study of their work, because the Fund does not ordinarily make grants: it is a research foundation which commissions studies and publishes the results. Finding the Geneva group not averse to having a book written about their efforts, so long as they were given funds to explore their prospects, Mr. Heckscher and his board of trustees decided to give a grant as "seed money" to the International Schools Examination Syndicate (as it was then called) and to engage me to participate in the organization's program and then write about it.

Nothing resembling a budget had been drawn up by the International Schools Examination Syndicate at the time when the grant was sought, and it was understood that some fairly definite if general allocation of the funds should be worked out before payments were made. On further consideration, Mr. Heckscher decided that I had better participate in the budget-making as the representative of the Twentieth Century Fund, and he suggested to I.S.E.S. that budgetary requests be cleared with me.

In retrospect, the arrangements among the Fund, I.S.E.S. and myself seem patently unworkable. As an observer who was going to write about the project, I was clearly a threat to what was admittedly and inevitably a weak organization. As an observer with an undefined brief from the source of the money, I was more than a threat: I was a hazard. During the spring of 1965, while I was resident in Geneva to work on and observe this project, I.S.E.S. suffered a major staff crisis in which my intervention was required. Organizational relations between myself and the Geneva group were cool from the start and worsened with the passage of time; in some instances personal relations were affected by the general tension. After the leadership of I.S.E.S. changed in the summer of 1966, and the project came under the highly competent direction of the Oxford University Department of Education, both organizational and personal relations between myself and the organization in Geneva were vastly improved.

Nevertheless, I have felt under some constraint in writing that fraction of this book which deals directly with the development of the examination in the period before mid-1966. Where hindsight now reveals errors in positions I once supported (for example, on the potential utility of an international examination to the educational systems of the developing countries), I find it difficult to exercise against myself the full resources of criticism. And where experience has demonstrated the errors of positions I opposed as they were taken, I feel a strong reluctance (quite apart from a natural dislike for breaking butterflies, or even moths, on wheels) to use my access to print to repeat at the end arguments which were rejected or ignored upon their presentation *viva voce* at the beginning. There are some pages where I have frankly felt it necessary to exercise extreme care to keep my comments from being influenced by what was, on balance, a distasteful personal experience.

By no means all of the experience was distasteful, of course. I am grateful for the understanding and help given by M. Martin; by Jean Siotis, chairman of the examining board of what has been rechristened as the International Baccalaureate Office and assistant professor at the Institut des Hautes Etudes Internationales; by Asmy Nawar, then chairman of the mathematics department on the English side of Ecolint and by his predecessor Mrs. Elsie Houwenstine; by John Sly of the International Schools Services in New York City; and by A. D. C. Peterson and William D. Halls of the Oxford University De-

Introduction

partment of Education. I am grateful, too, for the assistance given by Mrs. Ruth Bonner, secretary of the International Baccalaureate Office, in a situation designed to foster conflicting loyalties; for the courtesies of Eugene Wallach, the first executive secretary of I.S.E.S., plunged into an impossibly difficult situation not of his own making; and for the hospitality of Robert Leach, chairman of the Ecolint history department.

2

The work on this book, performed between late 1964 and mid-1967, involved visits to schools, universities and ministries of education in Argentina, Austria, Belgium, Brazil, Chile, Denmark, France, Ghana, Great Britain, Greece, Guatemala, Israel, Italy, Liberia, Luxembourg, Mexico, the Netherlands, Nigeria, Spain, Sweden, Switzerland, Turkey, the United States and Uruguay. Time was heavily concentrated in Europe, which offers most of the significant multinational schools and most of the universities both difficult of access and desired by the students.

There are some gaps in the coverage. No visits were made to Asian nations east of the Mediterranean shore, partly because Asian universities will accept students with any European certificate, partly because most Asian countries forbid their own nationals to attend international schools on their territory, and partly because the great majority of international schools in Asia are almost exclusively American in student population, at least in the secondary years. The study also omits any consideration of schools for the children of military personnel on overseas duty, since they are devoted essentially to managing the transition of these children to and from other schools of the home country. The American system of military schools is very large, consisting of some 300 units spread over the non-Communist world and educating more than 200,000 American children; but it does not in any sense offer an "international education."

More seriously, almost no attention is paid in these pages to either the proprietary boarding schools (which are what the words "international school" usually connote to upper-class Americans) or the church-related schools, most of which are also boarding schools. In part, the neglect of these schools stems from their exclusion from the International Schools Association of Geneva, the original sponsor of the International Baccalaureate plan. To the extent that this study was tied initially to the activities of the Geneva organization, the schools chosen for inclusion had to be those which had contact with Geneva. In addition, however, the few proprietary and church boarding schools which I did visit as the focus of the study expanded seemed to show little interest in the possibility of an international examination. The need for fashion, or for loyalty to both a faith and a sponsoring nation, seems to diminish concern with technical questions in international education; moreover, many religious schools have established relations with religious universities, providing a safe and approved channel by which their graduates can move to higher education.

The situation of the students at a private boarding school away from their home country is not, after all, a matter of any great moment. These students could just as easily be at school at home, and if their parents choose to endanger their chances of university entrance by sending them abroad to a school which does not prepare them for the necessary domestic examination, the problem is familial rather than societal. Nevertheless, some private and church-related schools are compelled to face the special difficulties of arranging the transition from one or at most two national secondary programs to uni-

Introduction

versities in many countries. Some of them are strong schools. It is a weakness of the International Baccalaureate project that the possible participation in the proposed examination by church-related and proprietary boarding schools has never been explored, and of this report that the needs and capabilities of these schools are not more extensively examined.

With this one important exception, there was good reason to concentrate on two varieties of schools: those sponsored essentially by the resident foreign community of the place where they are situated and those sponsored in part by governmental and intergovernmental agencies. It is to the children whose parents are sent abroad by their employers that society owes special attention; and it is on behalf of these temporarily expatriated communities, growing with the growing needs of international trade, diplomacy and charity, that a strong argument can be made for the larger allocations of money and talent which will be required if a successful international examination is to be built.

3

Approximately half of this report is devoted to the schools themselves, partly because the ultimate feasibility of an international examination depends upon the schools, partly because the first reason for trying to create such an examination is the needs of the schools. The intellectual puzzle of reconciling the academic programs of different cultures is a rewarding pastime and ultimately important, but it was not what the founders of the International Baccalaureate plan set out to do. (And as a practical matter there is no very strong case to be made for world-wide uniformity of pedagogical approach to any given subject matter, with the possible exception of foreign languages.) The quest for an international examination began at one hard-pressed school and was taken up in other quarters not as an exercise in international cooperation but because existing national examination requirements cripple even the most imaginative efforts to offer a single secondary program to children from a variety of cultural backgrounds.

Anyway, examinations do not exist *in vitro*. Their function at the end of secondary school is to certify that the results of a student's prior education are sufficient to yield a probability of success in higher education (or in the range of jobs for which in Europe the passing of the examination provides a necessary credential). Any examination which certifies work below the standard actually expected by the universities will be unacceptable at the admissions office (and in the modern world, of course, all secondary schools must sell into a buyers' market). An examination which cannot be passed by the graduates of the schools will draw no candidates. Thus the quality and flexibility of the schools are central questions; and schools are interesting institutions in themselves.

There is — or should be — a strong American national interest in the success of multinational schools. Adding together rather tentative data from the International Schools Services in New York City, the British Council in London and the French Ministry of Foreign Affairs, there would seem to be roughly 400 non-military schools which were established at least in part for the benefit of the children of a temporarily expatriated community. Students at these schools, counting the local residents who form the majority at most French lycées and at British and some American schools in Latin America and Africa, must number at least 250,000 (most of them at primary school ages). About half this total would be American. And the impact of these schools on the home community is larger than the figures indicate, because the group turns over every two or three years. At a guess, one American child in every hundred will have some experience of a school abroad. These children are not a random sample of their age groups: they are drawn very largely from the intellectually, economically and socially prominent families. Many of them are the sort of children who, as we have been told ad nauseam by public and private educational fund-raisers, constitute a vital national resource.

In most places, the American contingent is in fact large enough to sustain its own school. One can conceive of programs of governmental and corporate investment in American community schools abroad, and programs facilitating the transfer of teachers back and forth between such schools and the best American suburban systems, which would be sufficient to meet the needs of the American children on the scene. Indeed, while everyone talks internationalism, the trend of the last half-decade has been toward the Americanization of "international" schools which formerly educated a wider sample of mankind's children.

The guidelines for grants at such schools, established by the Office of Overseas Schools in the U. S. State Department, give preference to schools which serve the indigenous population and third-party nationals as well as the American community. But the meaning of this priority has not been analyzed in Washington. Even a good high school, strictly American in program, offering only what is required by, say, the State of Illinois for an academic diploma, will necessarily be restricted to serving the American and perhaps the Canadian communities, a few Israelis and Yugoslavs, and some local children on scholarship who would otherwise not be able to attend secondary school at all. But a preliminary request to the State Department for assurance that schools participating in the International Baccalaureate would not jeopardize their United States government grants produced a remarkable letter from the Bureau of Educational and Cultural Affairs:

"Schools which we help," wrote Frank S. Hopkins, director of the Bureau's Office of U. S. Programs and Services, "must have sufficient American influence to demonstrate American education to host-country nationals if the intent of Congress is to be realized.... Given the terms of reference under which we operate, we cannot assist schools which do not adhere to the accepted American educational pattern. If, in the future, American colleges recognize the international matriculation exam as a basis for admission and secondary education is reoriented toward preparing students for the exam, it might be possible to review our standards for aid. At this time, however, it seems unlikely that overseas schools adopting the new system can continue to qualify for grants." On further application, Hopkins' superior, Harry C. McPherson, Jr., said that the matter would be attended to, but no subsequent official letter on this problem has ever been received by anyone in any way associated with the International Baccalaureate Office — and McPherson is no longer with the State Department.

Naum Mittleman of the Lincoln American School of Buenos Aires, contrasting the difference in reception of his students and those of the local French lycée at the University of Buenos Aires Faculty of Exact Sciences, urged a visitor to persuade the United States government to negotiate with the Argentine government a treaty similar to that which gave Argentine recognition to the *baccalauréat*. Mittleman, who also taught at the Faculty of Exact Sciences, knew that his students at the American school were at least as well equipped as those from the lycée to handle the university science program; but there was nothing he could do to get them admitted. The United States government cannot in fact make such treaties, because American universities are autonomous; not only is the government unable to offer a quid pro quo in terms of university admission, it lacks even a mechanism for extend-

Introduction

ing "official recognition" to the Argentine *bachillerato*. Yet in the absence of such treaties American secondary schools abroad can hardly "demonstrate American education to host-country nationals," because host-country nationals who hope to continue to university cannot attend the schools. The only road out of the dilemma is American participation in an international program designed and operated by people of sufficient sophistication to see the acceptance of the international certificate by key American universities as the equivalent of official approval elsewhere.

To handle a program of this sort, the American overseas schools would have to be prepared to offer a thirteenth year to a number of students (not to all: those now up to College Board Advanced Placement work in senior year could complete the requirements in twelve). Most of the schools would have to greatly expand their library and laboratory facilities, and employ additional, highly qualified staff. They would also have to be willing to fight through with some parents the argument that they are *not* public district schools for all the American children of the locality but high-level college preparatory schools serving an international clientele in English.

The advantages of internationalizing American overseas schools would be more than just educational. Nobody can measure what French foreign policy has gained through a cultural relations program soundly based on a first-rate French school in the locality. Despite a good deal of unintelligent propaganda from both proponents and antagonists of "American methods," the United States has much to offer anywhere in the world in its systems for acculturating the young of the species. That these systems are consonant with high standards of work by adolescents has been dramatically demonstrated. Indeed, the demonstration has been made internationally: P.S.S.C. physics is now available in Russian, Swedish and

Spanish translations, and was encountered by this observer in (somewhat clandestine) use at the French lycée in Santiago de Chile.

No project for an international examination can hope to succeed without American participation and support. All of us — it goes without saying, in an idiom common to most languages — are committed to world peace and understanding, to international relations of unspeakable felicity, to the brotherhood of man and to good manners. Nevertheless, the fact remains that governments are more likely to take actions which serve national interests than actions which are wholly international in their purposes. The French have not made their heavy investments in overseas lycées because their charitable instincts override practical considerations. The strengthening of American schools abroad is clearly in the highest interests of the United States, which also stands to benefit from curricular changes that make these schools suitable depositories for children of other nationalities. To the extent that the State Department encourages the development of multinational programs and a multinational examination, the fairly gloomy trends reported in this book can be arrested and reversed; to the extent that the State Department ignores or even encourages the tendency of American parents to demand purely American schools, the opportunity to create multinational schools on an American base will be lost.

In this area, as in so many others, very different decisions can be defended with good arguments. What cannot be defended is the failure to make decisions — or even to know that they are necessary. The purpose of this book is to call attention to a small but not trivial problem which is likely to become important in the years ahead.

PART ONE

THE PROBLEM

CHAPTER 1: **The Education of Foreigners**

Ours is a century of transiency. Mass movements of mankind, tribal expansions, outpourings of refugees are not our invention, but systematic transiency is. In the seventh decade of the twentieth century, about two and a half million people, half of them American, are residing temporarily, on missions of one, two or three years' duration, in places far from the homes to which they will presently return. Many of them have children. This report deals with aspects of the education of their adolescent children, especially at the age when university entrance (or "college admission") has become the prime focus of schoolwork.

The great majority of the transient community have been sent abroad by the action of others, to meet national political or economic objectives or to serve an organized humanitarian desire. Many, perhaps most, have left home because the job they have or want to have, in diplomatic or military service or in a private enterprise with far-flung branches, requires this temporary expatriation. Only the military leadership, however, can absolutely command. For the other transients — considerably more than half the total — residence abroad is at least to a degree a matter of choice. In the absence of adequate facilities for the education of children, this choice will be made mostly by the very young or old, the childless, the spinster of either sex. A lack of acceptable schools hinders the recruitment of able and experienced people for international work in most areas of the globe.

Definitions of an acceptable school are almost as various as the people who make the definitions. The Chilean secondary schools, with their heavy emphasis on rote memory and the parroting back of answers to examination questions, are perfectly satisfactory to the great majority of the employees at the United Nations regional center in Santiago de Chile, for this is the Latin American pattern and the great majority of those who work for the U. N. in Santiago are Latin American. On the other hand, it was a national of adjacent Belgium who found the schools of Luxembourg so inadequate that he convinced the chiefs of state of Western Europe that the success of the Coal and Steel Community (and later of the Common Market) would require "European schools" for the children of the civil servants the economic organizations wished to recruit. And in Geneva few of the elite community of French nationals will patronize either the French-speaking schools of the canton or the French section of the International School of Geneva; they send their children to the Catholic school at Florimont or across the border to a French government lycée in Annemasse. A new French government-sponsored "international school" in Ferney-Voltaire may on its opening in 1970 take over this and other functions.

Obviously, the problem is most severe in the underdeveloped countries, where the solutions pioneered in the nineteenth century — mission schools and compound schools — are no longer viable. "Americans in India," writes the American sociologist Ruth Hill Useem, ". . . expect their children to receive an education which will prepare them for college. There are in India a variety of schools sponsored by American and international groups, but none offers an educational experience comparable to that found in the average suburban Stateside public school. None has yet developed the flexibility in timing and curriculum that can allow each child of this highly mobile population to have an orderly development in his education. Schools which have been adequate in the past have failed to keep up with post-World War II educational developments in the United States; many have inadequately trained teachers and poor facilities. Indian schools have long waiting lists and cannot accommodate to the differences in educational systems."[1]

Sociologists of other nationalities could make similar or more serious complaints. "In Dutch education," says Jan Van Der Valk, who runs the International School of The Hague and also the Netherlands' first comprehensive high school, "there is a certain *breath* — a certain atmosphere which Dutch people living abroad hate to lose." Even the French, whose incomparable chain of overseas lycées represents the world's most efficient investment of funds in the conduct of diplomacy, may find themselves in a country like Turkey or Iran, where the official French-financed schools are not permitted to accept French nationals. (And even officially approved schools may be considered dubious in some respects. "I recommend to parents with intelligent children who want to study science," says Edouard Morot-Sir, French cultural consul in New York City, which has a distinguished — but private —

[1] "The American Family in India," *The Annals*, Vol. 368, November 1966, pp. 144–5.

lycée, "that they should go back home for the last two years.") Where the local schools are conducted in a language which is not English, French or Spanish, or perhaps Russian, German or Italian, parents refuse to add to their childrens' burdens the perfection of a tongue which is unlikely to be of use to them later. Where the local schools operate in a European language and are of high quality — as is true of the best schools in West Africa — the local governments often will not deprive their own children of places to make room for foreigners.

At a meeting in Paris in early 1967, Albert Legrand, a Belgian administrative officer of UNESCO who is also an officer of the Federation of International Civil Servants, threatened to make the world-wide inadequacy of educational facilities for foreign nationals a matter for bargaining between the international organizations and their staffs. "When you recruit someone for an assignment," he said, "his first question is always, What is the school for my children? His second question is, Where do we live? But his first question about the housing is, How near is it to the school?" Echoing these remarks, G. H. Hoffman of CERN, the European nuclear research condominium, announced that his laboratories within a few weeks had received refusals from three significant scientists whose arrival had been eagerly awaited, because the scientists were unwilling to place their children in the available schools. The three cities involved in the CERN projects are Geneva, Trieste and Vienna: the problem is not restricted to backward areas.

FROM
THE CLASSROOM

In the compound of the University of Ibadan in Nigeria, about half a mile from the main buildings of the university (itself half a dozen miles from the city's noisy, demountable market), there

The Education of Foreigners

stands a small complex of modern residences, an air-conditioned suite of offices and a three-story classroom block housing the work area of the International School of Ibadan. The school — built mostly by the U. S. Agency for International Development and the Ford Foundation, on land donated by Nigeria's Western Region — is here to serve the university, and all the children come either from families which have some connection with this proud simulacrum of an English institution or from the foreign colony in the capital city of Lagos, where both the good secondary schools are reserved for Nigerians.

Of the 280 students at Ibadan in the autumn of 1965, about 100 were Nigerian, about 120 were American, about 20 were British, 15 Israeli and a dozen Lebanese, the rest of assorted nationality. Forty per cent or so were boarders (at annual fees of about $1,200), most of them returning home for weekends. The program being taught led to the West African School Certificate, granted separately in each subject to students who pass examinations closely modeled on the British examinations for the General Certificate of Education. Three slightly different versions of the exam are prepared, for Ghana, Nigeria and Sierra Leone, but they are considered equivalent; certificates are transferable from one country to another — and to Britain. Though Ibadan is in Nigeria, the program at the International School is based on the Ghanaian version of the exam, because the Ghana school year ends in June while the Nigerian year ends in December. (Seasonal differences are trivial in Nigeria, which is always hot and wet.) The staff at Ibadan in 1965 was almost equally divided between British, Americans and Nigerians; four teachers were directly supplied by the United States government through the Agency for International Development, at salaries considerably higher than that of the headmaster.

In this class an American girl is working with 21 children about 12 years old, the youngest group in the school. (Ibadan runs on a British grammar school pattern.) A trim Southerner, she is easily at home in the modern classroom with its aluminum-frame windows and vinyl-tile floor, and probably at home, too, in the heat that hangs in the air on both sides of the windows. About two-thirds of the class are Africans, English-speaking in theory but in most cases not in their homes, and the subject is (what else?) punctuation and capitalization. It is a real middle-class group of children, mildly obstreperous, a little fresh. On the blackboard, in a neat American schoolteacher's hand, is written: "apples, figs, and nuts." The teacher says, "That second comma can be left out; it's correct either way."

A girl volunteers, "Or you can say 'apples and figs and nuts' " — a little chant, very nicely done — "and leave out all the commas."

"Yes," says the teacher, "but that would be boring."

The literature text for this period is Rex Warner's *Men and Gods*, and the class has written papers on Baucis and Philemon and on why Icarus died so young. There is a little discussion of capitalization in titles: "If it's the last word, doesn't matter what the word is, you have to capitalize it." Then there is a somewhat longer conversation on capitalization in the body of the paper:

"When we're talking about the one God that we all believe in," the teacher says patiently, "then you capitalize it. But the gods you read about in Greek mythology — those you don't capitalize."

An African girl, pert in long pigtails, objects: "But what if you *do* believe in them?"

"Now," says the teacher, wearing a little thin, "we've been over this before. *Nobody* believes in them any more."

"*I* believe in them," says the little African girl.

The teacher can reply only, "Well, nobody *else* believes in them."

2

It is almost impossible to discuss the advantages or disadvantages of an "international" education without some agreed-upon definition of the word education and some knowledge of the child and his family. By common consent, travel is broadening; and the expansion of the child's horizons is surely

The Education of Foreigners

a prime goal of education. There are children sufficiently able and secure that they can simply move into the public school system of any modernized country to which their parents are sent. They can function this year in English, next year in Norwegian, three years from now in French, emerging from their experiences polylingual and perhaps equipped with a wider variety of approaches to common human problems. Language is not in most cases an overwhelming difficulty: most normally bright children, even at high school age, seem able to operate in a new language in school within six to nine months. The head of a French lycée once told the English Admiral D. J. Hoare, now headmaster of the international "Sixth Form" Atlantic College in Wales, "If the boy has brains and you have two years, don't worry about language."

But education in the modern world is also a profoundly nationalizing experience, giving a child a foundation in the culture of his future. For many children, moving to a school conducted in a language not their own in a place not their own is a trauma — and one in which parents are likely to be of even less than usual assistance, because they have their own troubles. If the child goes to the ordinary school of the locality, he is unlikely to find a teacher who will take the extra time needed to manage the adjustment of the stray foreigner who has wandered into (and may be "holding back") her class of locals.

Where large enough numbers of any one foreign nationality are involved, parents will try to ease the difficulties of their children (and make themselves more comfortable) by establishing a community and a school like home, centering on instruction in their own language. In these situations, it seems likely that the children's academic progress can be fairly smoothly forwarded: the one serious study of the question that has been made showed that United States Army children who had received at least two years of their education at overseas posts were on return to domestic schools very slightly ahead of a matched sample of Army children who had never left home.[1]

Some teachers and administrators feel that whatever the tests may show, children lose a great deal when they go abroad, even when they find in their new home a school which teaches in their old language. The *recteurs* and *proviseurs* of the French overseas lycées — who disagree with one another about most issues in politics and education, and are a living tribute to the French belief in individualism — unite in the statement that the children who come to them from metropolitan France are less successful in the (wholly French) academic program and less well behaved than the children native to the locality, who speak French only at school. "Our children are living in an artificial situation," says Donald Bullard, head of the American School of Madrid and formerly director of the foreign student program at New York University and architect of the Fulbright program in Italy. "They're part of a foreign colony, not part of Spanish life. They lack a *civic* sense, the kind of social sense you get just by living in a community." An Englishman who has taught at international schools on three continents and likes the work intends to return home when his oldest child reaches school age, "because I've seen too much of what happens to children who grow up abroad."

Still, parents feel, doubtless correctly, that all these problems are least severe when the expatriate community runs its own school in its own language. The French lycées, though now instrumentalities of the Ministry of Foreign Affairs,

---

[1] John W. Evans, Jr., "The Effect of Pupil Mobility Upon Academic Achievement," *National Elementary Principal*, Vol. XLV, No. 5, April 1966, pp. 18–22.

mostly began as cooperative ventures by French parents in a strange place. The great Greek diaspora has spotted Greek-language elementary schools throughout East Africa. When the sun was never setting on the British Empire, the English established schools for their private colonies in Florence and Athens, in Buenos Aires and Mexico City, as well as in the possessions of the Crown. Today, the American oil and mining companies move American education bodily to the desert and the bush; du Pont, coming into Luxembourg, set up a school with the curriculum of the school system in Wilmington, Delaware (but with teachers recruited from the ranks of the Luxembourgers). The American military, of course, creates wherever it goes "dependent schools" which are part of the great PX community.

Except for the military establishments, most such schools become, willy-nilly, "international," in terms of student population. Especially in countries which do not speak one of the major world languages, diplomats of all countries, staff members of international agencies, businessmen abroad will opt for a French or English or American school rather than for the local system. Where school keeps in one of the major languages, the international community is more likely to send children to the local establishments: in New York, London and Paris, the great majority of foreign children are enrolled in the ordinary domestic schools, public or private. Even here, however, many parents like the idea of a school which knows the problems of transients and will make special efforts to "receive" children who do not speak the language.

Especially where no one national community is large enough to sustain a separate school, efforts may be made to create a deliberately international school, which will not be tied to the requirements of any one culture. When Americans are involved, the effort is often idealistically motivated, expressing a desire to welcome in any feasible way children of all nationalities. But the charmingly named "American International School" is usually just as American in its orientation as the more accurately named "American Overseas School," which may have just as many nationals of other countries within its gates. The significant distinction on the scene is usually the presence or absence of *local* children, whose parents can count on significant political assistance when they fight for at least obeisance to cultural needs other than those of the nationality sponsoring the school. The French Lycée of Vienna, wholly financed by the French government but serving a student body most of which is Austrian, emits a far more international aura than the self-described international school of the same city, which is dominated by the American population and enrolls only a handful of Austrians.

There are a few schools which can be called international by any definition. Some of them, like the schools at Ibadan and at the Swedish-operated iron mines in the Liberian hills, have been called into existence by the need of a private or national organization to recruit skilled personnel from all over the world. Most of them, however, are the creation of an international organization. The outstanding examples are the International School of Geneva, founded to serve the children of League of Nations employees; the United Nations International School in New York City; and the six Scholae Europaeae established by the European Community to serve the needs of personnel of the Common Market.

FROM THE CLASSROOM

At the former NATO lycée at Saint-Germain-en-Laye, today struggling to achieve internationalism despite the departure of the NATO headquarters which used to supply the children, J. Du-

The Education of Foreigners

mont taught a "reception class" for secondary students — all ages from 11 to 16 — who arrived at the school without French, or without enough French to join what was at bottom a normal French program. He had these children with him all day, and took them through mathematics lessons, geography lessons, science lessons, even some history — all in French, the purpose being not to teach mathematics or geography or science or history but the use of the language in school. In the autumn of 1965 there were 24 children in the class, in a modern, rather small room with two large blackboards. They had been with Dumont seven weeks. The track record was that 15 or so would be ready for standard French lycée classes in another six or seven weeks, half a dozen others might require six months, and one or two wouldn't make it at all.

An unprepossessing man in early middle age, Dumont himself spoke only French and Italian; but in the words of E. Scherer, the *proviseur* of the school, he was "a genius at what he does." In 1965, he had been at it for fourteen years, which had not in the least diminished the extraordinary flow of energy he directed toward the children, all day long. Though his students could communicate with him only in French, because he had nothing else to offer them, he could communicate with them through an infinite variety of gestures and facial expressions, and a great gift for drawing scenes on the blackboard.

At this instant in time the class is running through Volume II of the Hachette *Cours de Langue et de Civilisation Françaises,* and Dumont is calling on each member of the class — "Tom, Dmitrios, Christian, Klaus, Björn, Paul Olafsen, Smeeth" — to answer questions from the book:

"*Le numéro neuf?*"

"*C'est un renard,*" says a girl of about thirteen.

"*C'est probablement un animal stupide.*"

"*Non,*" says the girl, "*c'est un animal rusé.*"

Then Dumont turns and draws an ocean scene on the board, a boat in the waves, on a distant shore a hill with a forest. This takes about five minutes, during which the children watch as any group, young or old, will watch an artist creating a landscape before their eyes. The scene is explained, and then all sorts of questions are asked about it:

"*L'Atlantique. C'est masculin ou féminin?*"

"*Masculin.*"

"*Naturellement.*"

We move inland. Where does *le peuplier* grow? After some pulling and hauling ("*Il faut corriger!*"), we get "*Au bord des rivières.*" Is the poplar broad? No, it's high. Opposite? "*Bas.*" Feminine of bas? "*Basse.*" "*Bon.*" The climate is humid. Opposite? "*Sec.*" Feminine of sec? "*Sèche.*" "*Bon.*"

Attention! *Sèche* is also a shellfish. And we have *chaine* — a *chaine* of mountains is not the same thing as a *massif*; different from the oak tree. He writes on the board "*Le gland est le fruit du chêne* (m)."

Again, "*être.*" A problem. "*Nous sommes tous des êtres humains, je suppose* . . ." Must be distinguished from *l'hêtre*, which is some damned tree. Similar problem. The judge does not "*faire la justice.*" That would be — Dumont draws his hand across his neck. The judge does "*rendre la justice.*" And not only the judge, of course. We have St. Louis rendering justice under an oak in the forest of Vincennes, Louis XIV rendering justice while walking in the garden of Versailles, Napoleon rendering justice while on his horse....

3

Any school located in a country where people speak a language other than the child's own can introduce him, as purely academic courses never can, to the meaning of proficiency in a foreign tongue. In some societies, indeed, it is not even necessary for the school to offer the language: Jan Van Der Valk of The Hague says that the schools he supervises don't teach Dutch because "all the children pick it up anyway. They want to *know* Dutch, they just don't want to study it." French children at the Französischer Gymnasium in Berlin become

The Education of Foreigners

fluent in German, though all their schoolwork is in French; and even in situations as isolated as those of the American schools of Paris, Rome and Vienna, where the school building is remote from the city and the children ride to a carbon copy of an American suburban school on special buses in which everyone speaks English, those who remain three years or longer usually become at home in the local language.

The promotion of this objective varies greatly from school to school. Even in so favorable a situation as that of the International School of Geneva, which has both a French and an English section, Americans are often astonished to find that on the English side French is just another "foreign language," usually taught by teachers who are not native speakers of French. An assistant headmaster of the American School of Brussels said, "You've got to teach the French that will fit a child for American examinations." In some American overseas schools, even in Italy and Germany, study of the local language is not required; and most French lycée students need never study the language of their host country. The English-Speaking School of Berne puts all its students through French rather than German, on the grounds that the Swiss German which serves the neighborhood is worthless if not harmful to them later, and the High German which would be useful in further education would make them unpopular locally. The American Community School in Athens, which at the request of the Greek government does not accept Greek nationals as students, does not require Greek; and only about 100 of the 800 students in the middle and upper schools take Greek.

Elsewhere, however, schools abroad see instruction in the language of the place as a first responsibility. Everybody at the American School of Rio de Janeiro takes Portuguese, though the school must battle university authorities in the United States to win acceptance for that language as a satisfactory course for entrance purposes. American schools in Beirut, Teheran and Kabul have made major efforts with Arabic, Persian and Pushtu, respectively; and the American School of Japan in Tokyo insists on Japanese to the point of boarding out students in the homes of Japanese who speak no English.

Full bilingualism is likely to be achieved in most situations only if the student must do at least some of his normal academic work in his second language. In several South American countries, this arrangement is compelled by law on the elementary level, and American children in, for example, Buenos Aires, must spend half their day working in Spanish just as the Argentinian children in the Lincoln American School spend half their day working in English. The now defunct NATO schools at Fontainebleau and Saint-Germain-en-Laye and the international school at Sèvres, all owned and operated by the French government, were established as French lycées with a difference, to teach foreign children primarily in French. At the United Nations International School in New York City, plans are afoot to create a fully bilingual atmosphere on an English base, with students required to take some standard academic work (probably history or geography) in French. The problems here are more difficult to solve than they seem on paper, because a school like UNIS must worry about substantial numbers of children whose native language is neither English nor French, for whom the requirement of functioning in two foreign languages may be a cruelty.

The model for the UNIS effort is the six Common Market European Schools, each of which brings together under one roof four linguistic "sections" — French, German, Italian and Dutch-Flemish. All French children must study German, all German children must study French, and those in the other sections have a choice of French or German. Non-academic hours — art, music, physical education — are run from an early

The Education of Foreigners

point in elementary school in a language not the child's own; and in the secondary school history and geography must be taken in a "vehicular language" different from that in which the student does the rest of his work. (Starting with the third year of the secondary program — the equivalent of the American eighth grade — all students in the Common Market schools must also take English as a foreign language.) For a brief period, the Schola Europaea in Brussels also demanded biology in a "vehicular language," but the requirement was dropped, the school's director explained, so as not to "punish the biology." To make bilingual accomplishment possible, the Scholae Europaeae offer in the early years of secondary education (ages 11 and up) as much as 12 hours a week of instruction in either French or German for students who are not yet prepared to begin studying history and geography in these languages. The methods employed rely heavily on tapes, slides, and language laboratories.

It seems clear enough that the educational values of bilingualism extend well beyond the mere mastery of a language. The relationship of patterns of thought to verbal formulations is a deep and mysterious subject on which psychologists are prone to dogmatize; but few doubt that a relationship exists. Almost every genuinely bilingual individual changes identity (often, startlingly, appearance) when switching from one language to another. Not only literature and history, but the inexact and exact sciences will be seen differently according to the linguistic frame into which they are fitted. There are options available to the bilingual child which cannot be opened for anyone imprisoned in a single language. In Russia and Poland, these options are considered so important that separate secondary schools operated entirely in a foreign language are available as part of the official state program; and among the most fashionable elementary schools in Paris and New York are (respectively) the Ecole Active Bilingue and the Ecole Française, both directed primarily to local children and both offering half of each day in English, half in French. To the extent that a school in a foreign place actually does create bilingualism in expatriated students, even fairly severe emotional problems resulting from the uprooting of the child can be justified by educational advantage.

And, of course, you never can tell what will be educational. Tourism itself, shoddy and predictable as it usually is, has been for many a flowing source of learning. Thus an American resident in Rome and not wholly happy with her son's formal schooling found that an Italian friend of hers was attempting instant archaeology at the construction site of a superhighway. The boy went off Saturdays to join the diggers for Etruscan relics, and came back one evening with a shard he tossed in his mother's lap. "You can keep *this*," he said scornfully. "It's medieval." The notion that this boy's education was held back because he went abroad could be entertained only by educators and psychologists (and perhaps parents). Contact with individuals of different cultural background — even (perhaps especially) from one's own country — is more likely while traveling, and the values gained by this contact, though easy to overstate, should not be ignored.

For the rest, the question of comparative advantage obviously raises the separate question of the quality of the school the child would have attended at home. For children from the underdeveloped countries, where education is still mostly highly formal, memory-based and snobbish, the experience of a school abroad is likely to be positive. (In the case of American schools, perhaps too positive: child-centeredness is a drug for children). For children who would otherwise be at Bronx Science or Oak Park or Taylor Allderdice, at the Lycée Henri IV in Paris or Merchant Taylors' in London or the Gladsaxe

The Education of Foreigners 33

Gymnasium in Copenhagen, the quality of instruction and the academic stimulation of the environment may be reduced by travel. In the English-language schools, quality has also suffered from the fact that the pedantic "progressives" in education were almost universally "internationalist" — that the UNESCO approach to the teaching of reading, for example, fell by default into the hands of the William Scott Gray look-say Dick-Sally-Jane tyrants. But doctrinaire bad teaching has been yielding to the pressure of middle-class parents, whose children come from the more ambitious schools back home — and to the youth of the teachers who can be drawn by the low salaries and minimal fringe benefits offered by American and English overseas schools.

One further claim is made for both the binational and the international schools. As "New Links," the fund-raising document of the short-lived International Schools Foundation, put it in 1957, "By enabling young people of many lands and races to work and play together in a spirit of friendly equality, these international schools are contributing to world understanding. The experience of children from different backgrounds and cultures having the common bond of being students together develops mutual respect and confidence. Identical aims and hopes emerge while the reality of difference and the value of diversity are acknowledged and appreciated." On the more limited scale of the Common Market schools, the claim is even grander. A document sealed into the foundation stone of each of the six Scholae Europaeae argues that "Having been brought up together and freed at an early age from the prejudices which separate peoples from each other, initiated into the beauties and merits of the different cultures, they will, as they grow, become conscious of their solidarity. While remaining fond and proud of their native country, they will become Europeans in thought, fully prepared to complete and consolidate the task undertaken by their fathers: the establishment of a united and prosperous Europe."

Apart from common sense and pious hope, the bases for such claims are hard to discover. In the international arena, acquaintance with people from other cultures — even friendships across cultural and racial lines — promotes empathy in some and antipathy in others, and we have no scale in which to weigh the balance.

The negative stories are, of course, the most dramatic. "The move to Vienna has been very hard on my son," said a Frenchman teaching at the lycée in Vienna. "After we had been here about six months he came to me one day and he said, 'The Austrians are no good. They have no history and no culture — no Molière, no Racine.'" At the Lincoln American School of Buenos Aires, most teachers feel that the children in the elementary division, who do half their work in Spanish with local children, become violently prejudiced against the Argentinians because of their resentment of the work load. At the International School of Geneva, everyone was delighted when students from the Arab countries agreed to contribute a page in Arabic to the school magazine, which actually got on press before anyone who could read Arabic saw it and informed the editors that the headline read, "Kill All the Jews!" In Lagos, a movement developed in the Parent-Teachers Association of the American school to eliminate the native contingent. "It's so hard for Americans to realize," said a Ford Foundation representative unhappily, "that African children steal."

"We were free of stereotypes when we started Atlantic College," said the wife of its headmaster. "But now! Imagine how Americans or Germans or Scandinavians should behave — they do."

There can be little question that many children strongly resist the internationalism flung at them in schools abroad. Though parental attitudes and individual personalities are certainly significant in determining which children become more tolerant and which more fierce in their prejudices, it also seems true that age plays a strong role. In the 10–11 area, and again in the 15–16 area, children from varying cultures seem especially resistant to anything which smacks of denationalization. Too few of the schools which deal with these children seem to understand that a child away from home needs to assert his identity as part of his national group, and that the nationality-based clubs and cliques which form at every multinational school are a necessary defense and not the machinations of some devil of misunderstanding.

Yet it is probably fair enough to say that people at multinational schools learn to live with each other even if they do not learn to like each other. By and large, the centrifugal forces in these schools are not cultural or political but technical and financial. The fragmentation of what were once joint Anglo-American ventures in Rome, Athens and Vienna occurred not because the English and Americans could not get along (though relations between the groups were often poor) but because the schools' resources were inadequate for the maintenance of separate programs and no single program could be found which met the needs of both groups. A crisis which almost tore the International School of Geneva into at least two schools in 1966 traced not to bad relations between its English-speaking and French-speaking sides (though deep currents of dislike ran between them) but to an inadequate financial management which had left the institution in a position where its leadership felt a need to sacrifice the French program for the benefit of the English program. The division of the lycée at São Paulo into two wholly separate schools at the secondary level — one of them French-international, the other entirely Brazilian — results from technical course requirements, not from national feelings.

Most multinational schools exist not because they are intrinsically desirable institutions, but because they are demanded by the personnel required for governmental and private jobs. But their very necessity provides an opportunity. For these schools, whether they wish to be or not, are laboratories, places where cleverness can discover and genius can implement the common core of education which is essential, regardless of cultural background, in the last third of the twentieth century.

To the extent that the experience of some nations can be helpful in solving the problems of others, the multinational schools offer splendid possibilities for cultural diffusion. To the extent that the educational systems of all nations are plagued with inherited irrelevancies, the multinational schools are ideally placed to strip away excess baggage. To make such experiments work will require investments of money, talent and time which are major from the point of view of the schools but trivial from the standpoint of the governments or intergovernmental agencies which must over the long run pay the bills. Before anything of significance can even be attempted, however, the schools must be assured institutional acceptance of the services they perform. The minutes of a 1967 meeting of the Educational Policies Committee of the United Nations International School note drily that "the school's obligation is first to get its students into the universities, not to experiment with the curriculum."

CHAPTER 2: **Access to Universities**

Intellectual parents, rightly or wrongly, tend not to worry too much about elementary school. "If the children are under ten," says Amos deShalit, director of Israel's Weizmann Institute, which recruits scientists for a year's visit, "the parents are usually willing to let them miss a year, to educate them at home or to send them to one of our schools, where of course they must take most of their time just learning Hebrew." For most parents, even the minimal parent-staffed compound school at an embassy will be satisfactory for the early school years.

Later the demands are much graver. Even if the parents' assignment is to a country with great universities, few are willing to risk the denationalization of the child which is an almost inevitable result of both secondary and higher education in a foreign country. "I am in this country ten years," said Jean van der Mensbrugghe, a Belgian working for the International Monetary Fund, explaining his interest in the establishment of an international school in Washington. "My daughter is now thirteen. If she goes to a U. S. high school she will have to go to a U. S. college and become American. I want her to have a choice."

Everywhere outside the United States, entrance to university is by special examination, centrally prepared and administered or centrally verified. In Britain the examining bodies are private "syndicates," or "boards" organized under the sponsorship of the universities, which are independent corporate entities; but a committee in the Ministry of Education meets to ensure parity among the examinations, and all the syndicates offer the same officially recognized General Certificate of Education at both "O" (Ordinary) and "A" (Advanced) levels.

In France until recently a single Office du Baccalauréat prepared a single set of examination papers which were offered throughout the nation (and in the overseas lycées); now each university sets an examination for its own region, but the Ministry of National Education keeps them all comparable. In Germany, each of the states makes its own arrangements for awarding the nationally recognized *Abitur*, but the national Conference of Culture Ministries coordinates the work. Often much of the examination is oral, and is conducted within the school by the school's own teachers, with a visitor assigned by the local Ministry of Education observing the procedure and sometimes throwing in important questions of his own.

All of these examinations serve primarily to validate the student's secondary education. Possession of the certificates is highly significant on the job market, and may be legally required for certain jobs, especially in public service. In most countries, passing these examinations guarantees admission to university, but in some, further examinations prepared by the universities themselves or even by individual faculties must also be surmounted before the student is accepted. The key word is "also" — nobody is admitted to the second run of examinations until he has got past the gatekeepers at the end of the first run.

In the United States, the situation is infinitely more complicated, because education is administered by fifty states rather than by a national government and because private institutions which may admit anybody still enroll about two-fifths of all college students. Some state universities are required (by law or even by the state constitution) to admit all applicants who have earned the diplomas awarded by high schools in their states without any noticeable supervision from higher authority. In New York State and Florida, admission to public university is controlled by performance on statewide examinations, which are directly related to the course work in New York and are more closely related to intelligence tests in Florida. In California, students are divided off by their rankings in their high school classes into those eligible for university colleges, those eligible for state colleges and those eligible for junior colleges.

Private colleges — and many state universities in considering applications from out-of-state students — rely on machine-scored multiple-choice aptitude tests, primarily on the College Boards prepared by the Educational Testing Service to the demands of the College Entrance Examination Board. Both organizations are private. The tests do not yield a passing or failing score but a comparative ranking of candidates, who now number almost one and one-quarter million a year. As a general rule, private institutions establish their own cut-off points: they may accept some students who score below these points on the College Boards, but it isn't likely. One state system (Georgia) has adopted these tests as its own criteria for university entrance, regardless of the recommendations of the high school the applicant attended.

Nobody is very happy with the existing selection procedures. In a world-wide study for UNESCO, Frank H. Bowles, formerly director of the College Entrance Examination Board, wrote that the examination systems "affect the validity of secondary school credentials, constrict the programmes of secondary education, choose students on the basis of small differences in their performance, reject students who are prepared to do the work of higher education, create examination burdens, and lead to the establishment of supplementary but undesirable school programmes."[1] But to the extent that the examinations are an evil, the situation grows worse not better every year; and there is no end in sight.

2

The years since World War II have seen a steady intensification of competition for increasingly scarce places in every nation's universities. In the United States by the mid-1960s, the median score on the verbal section of the Scholastic Aptitude Test of the College Entrance Examination Board had dropped from 500 to about 430 (thanks to a sixteen-fold increase in the number of candidates who, in the British phrase, "sit the exam"); but the median score of the freshman class at the nation's most prestigious colleges had risen from about 560 to about 620. (Because the scores are on a logarithmic scale, these differences are very substantial. The median candidate in the mid-1960s stood at about the 25th percentile of the group which took the tests in 1942. The median entrant to the Ivy League colleges in 1942, with his score of 560, was ahead of 70% of those who took the verbal S.A.T.; the median entrant in the mid-1960s, with his score of 620, outranked more than 90% of his competitors.)

In France, where possession of a *baccalauréat* was once an

[1] *Access to Higher Education*, UNESCO, New York, 1963, Vol. I, p. 38.

absolute guarantee of admission to any university, the Ministry of Education has now established a minimum mark below which the student receives a *baccalauréat* which qualifies him for a job but not for university. In Belgium, by the law of June 8, 1964, the *certificat* which once served as both a secondary-school diploma and a university entrance passport now admits only to a second, separate university examination. (The old *certificat*, says M. Leyvarlet, secretary-general of the Belgian Ministry of Education, grants "entry into life.") In Germany, where the federal constitution provides that the *Abitur* must be accepted for entrance at all universities, the faculties of medicine and engineering have quite illegally (but quite necessarily) imposed their own *numerus clausus*. In Britain, where the papers on the General Certificate of Education examination can receive five different passing grades, only the higher grades today carry absolute assurance of admission to even a "red-brick" municipal university.

Apart from the military non-coms and perhaps the construction workers, virtually everyone on international assignment insists on university education for his child. As recently as thirty years ago, the university was merely one of many routes to economic or social preferment in the Western countries. Today a degree or a license of some sort is the royal road, often the only road, to assured future status. American parents have been known to begin worrying about their children's college prospects at the time of entering them in a kindergarten.

At the international and overseas schools, university admissions pressure is felt at increasingly early ages. The French Lycée of London, which once had to begin special work for British examinations for local students only at the age of 17, must now offer English mathematics and practice at writing translation papers into English to students as young as 14. ("We try to keep the school socially together but academically separate enough to satisfy the national examination requirements," says Anthony Morgan, director of the English side. "It's a very simple goal but it becomes very complicated.") The International School of Geneva, which before World War II could operate primarily in French on programs largely of its own devising, must break its secondary-school population not only into virtually separate English and French schools but also into College Board or G.C.E. streams on the English side and *baccalauréat* or Swiss *maturité* streams on the French side. "Forty years ago international education was mostly international. Now it is mostly education," said Victor Schaller, who had been a teacher at the Geneva school from its beginnings in 1924 (and was encountered in 1965 drilling the school's sole class of Swiss 12-year-olds in the geography of the 22 — or 25? — cantons).

Changes in the nature of education have worked against the university admission chances of children going to school away from their home country. When school programs were predominantly classical and linguistic, sheer persistence was enough to produce survival at the examinations. Today's examinations measure skills more subtle and consequently more national in coloration than the mastery of Latin verb forms and basic Euclidean proofs. Both the people who write the questions and the people who correct the answers are unconsciously submerged in a culture which is not the immediate environment of the student abroad. The fact that the functions of designing and correcting papers are joined in the same man in the American "objective" test does not in the slightest relieve the overseas American of this handicap; indeed, the linguistic trickery which characterizes the great majority of the "objective" test "items" may mean that the American abroad taking his College Boards is more severely punished than the French student struggling with the questions on the *baccalauréat*. The French student's papers will probably be read by members of the French overseas community rather than by a metropolitan teacher, while the American student's pencil marks on the answer sheet will feed into the maw of the home computer.

"These children are terrifically handicapped on the College Boards," says Donald Bullard of the American School of Madrid. "The mother's Venezuelan, or the parents have turned the children over to servants. The movies, the radio, the street are all in Spanish. To handle the sort of question they get on the S.A.T. [Scholastic Aptitude Test] they have five hours of English a week — that's all."

In her study of the American family in India, Ruth Useem suggested that some Americans "try to plan their foreign assignments so they can be either in Europe or the United States when their children reach high school age." Those who are already in Europe find half this alternative unsatisfactory. Many of them will endanger their careers to get out of Europe and back home to protect the future of their adolescent children. Failing a transfer home, they will use the power of the American international presence to demand American College Board programs where they are — even if this bias makes these schools cruelly unsuited to the needs of the children of other nationalities who attend them. For, whatever may be the realities of education, the facts of institutionalized schooling require specific preparation for specific examinations.

FROM THE CLASSROOM

At Atlantic College in Wales, a "Sixth Form" two-year school for boys from all over the world who are finishing their secondary education, Tom Carter is taking a class of seven over the booby traps of past examinations for G.C.E. A-level French, which they are about to encounter. The school is located in a spectacular fifteenth-century castle on the Bristol Channel, one of the homes Hearst reconditioned for Marion Davies; to make it suitable for a school, Atlantic College had to rip out some of the establishment's thirty-six bathrooms. Across the hall in the old servants' area which serves as headquarters for Carter's foreign language department is a superbly equipped language laboratory, for which the extraordinary Atlantic College staff has prepared its own tapes. Though apparently very English, a straightforward, mildly ironical, dark-haired man in tweed jacket and flannel trousers, Carter is himself more than adequately international — Polish by birth, French- and German-speaking by residence as well as by study. In 1967, Carter moved on to the faculty of Southampton University, illustrating another world-wide problem — the tendency of an expanding system of higher education to get its faculty by robbing the secondary schools of their best teachers. Most of the rest of the staff is British, though many have summer places abroad. The school, while dominated by North European students (British, Irish, German, Scandinavian) and Americans, does recruit all over. Carter's favorite student in this French class was identified as "an Italian boy: his father is a Danish Jew, his mother an Arab."

The book under discussion is Gide's *La Porte Etroite*, and the question, drawn from a previous examination paper, is whether the "sacrifice" made by the leading female figure was *folie* or *sainte*. Carter draws a line down the blackboard, heads each side with one of the alternatives and solicits suggestions from the class. They come, mostly in English, sometimes in French, and Carter notes them down. Signs of impatience multiply: the class wants the right answer, not a list of contradictions to be used in an essay. Finally one of the boys asks, "What is the conclusion?"

"Wait a minute," Carter says in English. "Don't come to a conclusion before making your plan; you want to know how you're going to write it."

Finally the best answer comes: *"Ni l'un, ni l'autre."*

Another boy explodes: *"La question est ridicule!"*

Carter eyes him calmly. "*Toutes les questions,*" he says, "*sont ridicules, mon vieux*" — and then switches to English: "But it isn't your role to judge."

3

From the university side, there are three different but related problems, which should be looked at separately.

By far the most important is the question of foreign students who have gone through their own country's standard secondary course and now seek admission to a normal university program in another country. Angus Maddison has estimated that there were about 170,000 such students abroad in the early 1960s, with continuing rapid growth expected.[1] (For the United States a committee chaired by Ralph W. Tyler of the Center for Advanced Studies in the Behavioral Sciences wrote in 1964, "Our foreign student population has doubled in the last decade, and there are many indications that it will double again within the next decade."[2]) In fact, the rate of growth appears to have slackened considerably, because the universities cannot handle the load or the special problems — and because the sending nations have grown increasingly reluctant to ship their brightest young out of the country at an impressionable age. Everywhere, the proportion of university places occupied by foreigners dropped between 1961–62 and 1966–67; and in some countries, notably Austria and Switzerland, the absolute numbers fell.

For some African and Asian nations, the export of students has been little short of a disaster. The Tyler committee estimated that "as many as 40 per cent of all the students from

---

[1] *The Contribution of Foreign Skills, Training and Technical Assistance to Economic Development,* O.E.C.D., 1965, pp. 108–9.

[2] "The Foreign Student: Whom Shall We Welcome?" Education and World Affairs, New York, 1964, p. 2.

a certain Asian country stay permanently in the United States under one scheme or another."[3] The proportions that remain in France and in Britain are probably almost as high. The vast majority of foreign students are financed at least in part by remittances (governmental or private) from home, which means that their maintenance at university is a drain on the foreign exchange resources of the sending states. For both practical and prestige reasons, the "developing" nations have invested large budgets in the construction and staffing of their own universities, many of which (especially in Africa) are not used to capacity. While the home university must accept candidates who lack the full qualifications for entrance, it can scarcely approve of a policy which sends some of the best qualified abroad for their education — particularly in the face of the danger that those who leave will not return.

Parenthetically, it should be noted that both universities and governments are to be criticized for failing to foresee that it would be difficult to get the boys back on the farm after they'd seen Paree. To spend one's time in Europe was the mark of the aristocrat in most of the colonies; to have a child in Europe was the clearest assertion of status by the colonial parvenu. To the extent that meritocracy substitutes for and mimics aristocracy, the total loss of the expatriate student was highly predictable. Anyway, the desire of the educated African or Asian to remain in one of the world's metropolitan centers is simply an extension of his preference when home for a life in the capital city rather than a life in the backwoods — a preference which the political leaders of these countries obviously share.

For many students from developing nations, home offers no opportunity to use the sophisticated techniques that have

[3] *Ibid.*, p. 11.

just been learned. A particle physicist obviously finds little to do in Madagascar, and so does an economist who needs data to help make plans. Many of the new nations suffer also from what the American committee bluntly described as a "closed-opportunity structure or the inefficient social provision for the use of trained people, however badly they may be needed for social and economic development."[1] Particularly in situations where national loyalties are feeble, the wonder is not that so many have contrived ways to remain in the host countries but that so many have cheerfully returned home. (And it should be said that many of those students from the underdeveloped nations who remain in the United States may become available to their native countries again if these countries come to require large technically trained cadres. Both South Korea and Formosa have successfully recruited for new technical institutes.)

Despite the countervailing pressures at home, however, the demand for places for foreigners continues high at many universities. The size of the demand is initially a function of the language of instruction. There are as many foreign students (about 1,300) at the French-speaking University of Brussels, with a total enrollment of about 5,300, as there are in the entire Dutch-speaking university system of the Netherlands, with a total enrollment of about 70,000. More than half the students at the University of Geneva are of foreign nationality, while the percentage of foreign undergraduates at the University of Stockholm is negligible. Both the Netherlands and Sweden have launched English-speaking "institutes" for foreign students, but the recognition granted to Dutch and Swedish degrees by other nations does not extend to these institutes, and intergovernmental negotiations would be ne-

---

[1] "The Foreign Student," p. 11.

cessary to establish them. "Until now," Professor Suni Carlsen of Uppsala wrote in 1964, "the Swedish authorities have been reluctant to take part in such ventures. Instead they have started to give fellowships to students from underdeveloped countries for undergraduate studies in countries other than Sweden."[1] Admission to technology and medical faculties, moreover, is entirely reserved for Swedish students.

A second significant factor is the extent to which the student-importing nations have gone after such business. The maintenance of German as an international language, despite its exclusion from the United Nations, was a matter of prime importance to both Germanies and to Austria, which until recently made places available almost promiscuously: in 1961–62 more than a quarter of all the students in Austria, and about a tenth of the students in Germany, were foreigners. The global crusade for French culture includes a reservation for foreign students of about one in nine of the places in the crowded French universities, and the Russians have actively recruited in Africa for Lumumba University in Moscow — a grand tour of the Soviet Union, all expenses paid, and not much work expected. Though the proportion of foreign students in American universities is only one in fifty, the enormous university enrollments in the United States make it by far the leading importer of students, with more than 85,000 in either undergraduate or graduate studies in 1967.

Movement within Europe is simple. Among the achievements of the Council of Europe has been the short-circuiting of the old "equivalency" committees in the national ministries of education — official and persnickety consumer research operations which ruled on whether foreign secondary-school certificates were as good as the home product. By a European Convention signed in 1953, a citizen of any European coun-

---

[1] *The Intellectual Face of Sweden*, ERGO International, 1965, p. 57.

try who has passed the examinations which would make him eligible for university entrance in his own country is also eligible for admission to a university in any other European country. Only a minor amount of this transfer actually occurs, because most European nations will not accept foreign medical or legal or engineering or teacher training as adequate for any job requiring a state license. (Efforts to establish a European University in Florence fell through because such acceptances could not be secured.) The treaty has been a boon, however, to the Norwegians and the Greeks, whose domestic provision of higher education is far below the demand for it. These two countries send about a quarter of all their university students abroad, and on the whole recognize the certificates with which they return.

There are occasional annoyances — the Swedes, for example, were outraged at being required to accept at Stockholm a young man from Bulgaria who had passed his national examinations at the age of 16, though nobody in Sweden is permitted to go to university below the age of 18. Differences between the state-controlled continental universities and the independent British universities have also created an irritant, because no treaty governs what a British university can do. Until 1965, in fact, the University of London (to most Europeans the most desirable of the British establishments) would accept as the equivalent of the local G.C.E. A-level exams only a first academic degree from a foreign university — which in the case of German candidates means a doctorate. Rhodes Scholars, having completed their undergraduate work in America, have always been surprised to find themselves returned to undergraduate status at Oxford.

Transfers between former colonies and the former mother country are usually relatively easy. British Africa is dominated by a G.C.E. examination either administered directly from England (by London or Cambridge) or locally run but modeled on the English pattern and kept to an equivalent standard (by the West African Examinations Council, which links Ghana, Nigeria and Sierra Leone; or by the recently formed and struggling East Africa Examination Council.) Admissions to British universities from the Commonwealth countries are arranged by a special office established for that purpose. The secondary schools of formerly French Africa are staffed by teachers imported from (and paid by) metropolitan France, and an identical *baccalauréat* is offered. In the Middle East, the Lebanese *baccalauréat* is more papist than the Pope, honored in France — and available to perhaps two per cent of the Lebanese population. Spain accepts the *bachillerato* of all Latin American countries.

Movement to universities in the United States, Switzerland, Austria and Germany, or from educationally independent developing countries like Egypt, Iran, Taiwan and Korea, presents an enormous headache. In 1965, there were a thousand Iranians at the University of Vienna — "Some of them," said its *Rektor* despairingly, "don't even speak German." The University of Geneva in the mid-1960s began cracking down on Latin American and African admissions, where the track record was awful. "The question of *motive* is central," said its secretary, Bernard Ducret. "Why are they here? For a while there was a thought that the Swiss consular people might meet candidates — but the consuls have other things to do, and they aren't equipped for it."

In West Germany since the war, control of education is vested in the states rather than in the national government, but the universities themselves and the culture ministries of the states have formed associations to deal with the difficulty of selecting foreign students. (According to a representative of the Deutsche Akademische Austauschdienst, which coordinates the admission and scholarship programs of the universities, "they are not bound by what we say. It happens, not every day but every week, that they find some nice boy, they don't pay any attention to our recommendation, and they admit him.") The Standing Conference of Culture Ministries has developed a book of ratings of foreign secondary-school leaving examinations, which has been made available to authorities in other countries on a highly confidential basis. "We are already in trouble," says a spokesman for the conference, "because the Jordanians found that we gave a higher rating to the Israeli *Bagrut* than to their G.C.E." The special problems posed by students who arrive with the easily gained certificates of Iran and Egypt have been met straight-on in West Germany by requiring candidates from those countries to take in Germany a year of pre-university courses. "The Eygptians objected that this compulsory year was an insult," said a German *Rektor*. "I showed them the figures on how their students were doing."

The 2,300-odd American colleges are of course absolutely independent — *sauve qui peut* — in their admissions procedures. Harvard, which receives the most applicants, will accept "superior results on any government or centrally administered national examination . . . which would admit the applicant to a university of the highest standing in his own country. . . . A high level of performance . . . may entitle the student to [placement] . . . as a Sophomore or second-year student."[1] The ordinary Swiss cantonal *maturité* is thus in theory not acceptable to Harvard: only the federal *maturité*, which is taken by a tiny fraction of Swiss students at private schools, will be considered. (For this reason, a Swiss physics student who had won acceptance at the Polytechnical Institute in Zurich, one of the continent's half-dozen outstanding technical institutes, was recently turned down by both Harvard University and Massachusetts Institute of Technology, to

[1] "Information for Students from Abroad Interested in Harvard College," pp. 2, 6.

the bewilderment of the educational establishment of Switzerland.) Candidates from English-speaking Africa and India will be taken at Harvard only on presentation of British or British-approved documentation: no purely Indian certificate is acceptable — not even an Indian Bachelor of Arts degree. Delegates from the American organization Education and World Affairs have gone around English-speaking Africa rather wistfully suggesting to the local students that they take College Boards. "I urge my Nigerians, 'Don't do it,'" said David Snell while headmaster at Ibadan. "Don't compete with the Americans on their home grounds. Qualify as a foreigner."

Outside the major Eastern colleges, most of which have requirements similar to Harvard's, the standards for entry of foreign students tend to be considerably less severe — and highly erratic. The Tyler committee accepted reports "that many foreign students who have been rejected by institutions in their own countries because of low quality and potential have been admitted to the United States only to drift aimlessly from one institution to another. Unfortunately, a few American colleges catering to foreign students are tantamount to residential diploma mills. . . . In general, the lowering of standards of admission apparently places the U. S. faculty members in the perennial dilemma of having to decide whether to grant the so-called 'foreign-student C' or 'foreign-student M.A.' instead of a failing mark or the denial of a diploma. There is a strong consensus among those most closely involved in foreign student affairs that faculty members who practice a double standard to enable inadequately-achieving foreign students to pass through academic hurdles are doing high-quality foreign students a grave injustice, and also injuring the world reputation of American higher education."[1]

Many American colleges, for fund-raising and other reasons,

---

[1] "The Foreign Student," p. 13.

like the exoticism of students on campus from far places; nearly all feel that they are serving humanitarian purposes by offering places to the young of the underdeveloped areas. Only about ten per cent of the foreign students at American universities have been brought in under the selection procedures and the financial umbrella of the Fulbright program; the rest are privately sponsored in one way or another. Many should never have come, and many (perhaps most) spend their student years in America in financial want not far removed from destitution.

The generosity with which American colleges accept foreign students has not been matched, to say the least, by universities outside the United States considering American applicants. There are only a handful of places which will accept even students with the highest scores on the College Board aptitude and achievement tests (or, perhaps more relevant, top scores on the Advanced Placement examinations, which are roughly comparable to the European exams, subject by subject). At best, the European universities will take as entrants American students who have successfully completed two years at an American college. The desire of Americans to take at least part of their education overseas is most commonly met by summer courses or by the "junior year abroad" program under which an American college rents a residential house, retains basic supervision of its own students, and sends them to take some classes with the locals. In general, the European universities feel that the participants in these programs have been insufficiently screened, psychologically, linguistically and academically: far too many are tourists living on a cruise ship. ("There is also too much advertising use of the European name," says Maurice Harrari of Education and World Affairs.) The European universities' experiences with "junior year abroad" have by no means eased the plight of the American overseas schools which would like to have both an

American program and a fair proportion of non-American students.

FROM THE CLASSROOM

The French Lycée of London is part of the long-established Alliance Française, housed in a gigantic ugly modern building on Cromwell Road between the Victoria and Albert Museum and the Air Terminal. It is the largest school of its sort in the world — 2,300 students, from pre-kindergarten through the end of high school — and it is both socially and academically regarded as one of the best private schools in London. Up to age 14 all students, whatever their nationality, follow a standard French program in French; then those who wish to go to British universities begin to split off for increasing parts of the day. By the time the children are 16 or 17, the English side, about two-thirds of the school, is mostly separate from the French, and is housed in converted private residences around the corner from the main building. To keep the French side alive in the *classe terminale*, the lycée imports every year from metropolitan France, on scholarship, about ninety boys and girls — or, rather, young men and young ladies.

This class is on the English side, working toward the A-level examination in English literature, and of the sixteen students, twelve are English, two are French, one is Greek and one is Italian. The room is in a basement, and remarkably cold in November: all of the children are wearing heavy sweaters, and the teacher, a handsome, determined lady in horn-rimmed glasses, wears a leather jacket. The set play, required by the examination syllabus, is Shaw's *Saint Joan*, which is rather fun for all.

"What is Warwick's point of view?" the teacher asks, referring to the celebrated discussion between feudal nobleman and feudal bishop, who have agreed on the need to eliminate Joan.

A girl offers, "He's afraid the feudal aristocracy will be stopped and there will be only one King."

"And what is the threat Cochon sees?"

" 'Tis Protestantism, isn't it?"

"What does it point forward to, this scene? — because a scene is no good unless it points somewhere. . . ."

The girl says, "To her decline — to her ——"

"Yes?" says the teacher.

And the girl, to whom the story is very real, mutters, "Burning."

The class is interested in its visitor and wants to talk, especially about the nuisance of studying "French" for the purpose of passing G.C.E. "Up to last year," a boy says, "we never translated. It's difficult. Anyway, the exam doesn't give you the vocabulary you use."

A girl adds, "It's useful training if you want to be an interpreter, but not if you don't."

Another girl shakes her head. "I have no trouble translating from Italian to English or English to Italian, but it's very hard for me to translate between French and English."

Still, that's what they have to do, and they will do it: the examiners don't care about bilingualism, about the ability to function in French; they care about translating. The teacher says that after ten or twelve years of doing all their work in French they have even worse problems with English composition. Nevertheless, problems or no, they score well on the exams.

Closely related to the large problem of the foreign student who took his secondary education at home is the much smaller question of the foreign student whose secondary school was located neither in his home country nor in the country of the university he now wishes to attend. Trivial in terms of the quantities of students involved, this question is important as a possible entering wedge for a Nansen passport to universities: unlike most admissions questions, it will usually be resolved in the applicant's favor. Except in the case of Americans, the European universities will normally accept anyone who could be admitted in his home country on the basis of the piece of paper he secured abroad — and will probably accept anyone whose piece of paper would be valid if the person who held it were a national of the country that issued it, even though his home country does not accept it. The latter category takes a little explaining. The French *baccalauréat* is not accepted for university entrance in, for example, Brazil or Spain; but a Brazilian or Spanish student who acquired this document in France or in an overseas French lycée would probably be admitted by a Belgian or Swiss or Italian or German university. This arrangement has been useful primarily to the children of political exiles — especially the rare Spanish Republicans who have money.

By this short step we come to the third problem, which was the origin of this report — university admission for the student who has taken the last years of his secondary education abroad and now wishes to return home. Here, with exceptions (notably Sweden, the Netherlands and Israel), there are no "equivalencies" — in the Council of Europe Convention, all signatories specifically reserved the right not to recognize foreign documentation for their own nationals.

A French student with a *baccalauréat* will be accepted without much question at any American university; an American student with a *baccalauréat* will be told to take the College Boards, on which he will unquestionably suffer a penalty because he has done his secondary work in French rather than in English. And at many colleges his score on the College Boards will far outrank his possession of a *baccalauréat* when the admissions committee makes its decisions. This can also occasionally work the other way: a boy at the NATO lycée at Saint-Germain-en-Laye passed the first part of the French *bac* in 1964 (the last year of the two-part *bac*), but failed *Mathématiques-Elémentaires* in 1965. His math-science scores on the College Boards, however, were easily good enough to win him admission to the Colorado School of Mines.

Access to Universities

Really outstanding American students, of course, need not worry much about examination requirements, which American colleges can ignore whenever they please. In 1965 the French Lycée of London sent to Harvard a German and an American who had followed an entirely French program through excellent scores on *Math-Elém;* so far as the lycée knows neither boy took College Boards at all. For Americans who are merely capable, however, the problem is real; and in other countries the pieces of paper may be absolute.

A German student with an *Abitur* must by treaty be admitted to a French university; but a French student in the same German school who offers the same *Abitur* will not be accepted unless he can prove continuous residence in Germany for at least five years. A Swiss student with a *maturité* or an Austrian *Matura* will be accepted automatically at a German university, but a German student with the same papers cannot be accepted under any circumstances. As a spokesman for the West German *Rektorenkonferenz* put it to the writer, "We cannot permit rich people to send their children across the borders to schools which perhaps do not have the same standards as our own, and then demand university places for them." No length of residence abroad can excuse a German from an *Abitur.* The youngest son of conductor Wilhelm Furtwängler, who had become a Swiss citizen, took his entire elementary and secondary schooling in Switzerland, but when he wished to go to a German university, he was required to attend a German *Gymnasium* for two years beyond the *maturité,* to secure the standard German *Abitur.*

4

These regulations on the admission of nationals — complicated, often confused, sometimes idiotic — render almost impossible the creation of truly international secondary schools even in international centers. If each student must be separately prepared for the examinations of his own country, classes of mixed nationality are out of the question in the last years of the secondary program. Like the restaurant in the Bemelmans story, which offered on the menu the meat of all animals but told a patron who ordered elephant cutlet that the management could not kill its elephant for just one cutlet, an international school to remain financially healthy must limit the number of its real programs.

In a very few common-language areas, regional agreements have eliminated the problem. The nations of Latin America, by and large, recognize each other's *bachillerato* even for their own nationals; and the United States and Canada will accept each other's secondary-school certificates and examinations regardless of the nationality of the applicant. The French overseas lycée system has made the difficulty more or less manageable in many countries through binational treaties. (Exactly equivalent arrangements have also been negotiated by the Italian Foreign Ministry to make possible the operation of Italian *licei* in Argentina, Ecuador, France, Spain and the Union of South Africa.) The main purpose of these treaties is to ensure that residents of the city where the school is located can send their children to the lycée without any reduction of their chance for university admission. In Italy, Austria, Berlin, Argentina, Chile, Mexico — to mention only places visited during the course of this study — the treaties permit the lycée to teach a standard French program leading to a standard French *baccalauréat* which will be accepted by the local authorities as the equal of their own secondary-school certificate. Normally, if only for reasons of *amour-propre*, there is some minimal instruction in the local language and culture by teachers locally trained and licensed, and the final examination, in addition to the *baccalauréat* papers, includes a

Access to Universities

gesture in the direction of these hours of local teaching (usually three to five a week). In Austria, the course in "Austrian Traditions and Culture" is known with charming Latinity as *nostrificazione*.

A side benefit of these treaties, where they exist, is that they make it possible for, say, a Chilean to attend the French Lycée of London if his father is stationed there; to acquire in London a *baccalauréat*; and to return home armed with a document equal in value to the home-country *bachillerato*. (He must still, like all Chileans, take an entrance examination given by the faculty of the university in which he wishes to study; but experience has shown that this examination, which is not language-centered, is duck soup for the holders of a *baccalauréat*.) But the French have not by any means succeeded everywhere in selling the *baccalauréat* as a sufficient measure of capacity for university entrance. In Spain, Britain, Brazil, Sweden, Uruguay, the United States — to mention, again, only countries visited for this study — the lycée must also offer at least large pieces of the national program to prepare local children for the national examination. In Turkey and Iran, the treaty provides for the teaching of the local program in French, by teachers many of whom have been sent from France, the work to be sanctioned by an examination given in French which is not, however, the *baccalauréat* — and which will not be accepted in France for French students. Similarly, the German *Gymnasium* in Athens offers Greek students a "small *Abitur*" which is adequate to admit Greeks to German universities but will not admit Germans.

The eccentricity of the treaty arrangements creates amusing situations. Because all South American nations accept the Chilean *bachillerato* but many do not accept the *baccalauréat*, the international community in Santiago de Chile goes to the local schools while upper-class Chileans send their children to the beautiful new lycée to study in French. In Istanbul, the old and exclusive Galatasary Lisesi is entirely Turkish in pupil population (Turkish in nationality, anyway: at least half the students are described by the staff as Greek or "Israelite" in national background). The children of the French teachers at this school, and the rest of the foreign colony, must go to a little lycée in the compound at the French consulate, inadequate in every way, except that it prepares students for the standard *baccalauréat*. The French teachers at Galatasary donate their services to the lycée in the compound. Americans in Istanbul are even worse off, because Robert College makes no arrangements at all for them. "One reason American companies don't come here," said headmaster Robert Shirar rather complacently, "is that there's no school for their kids."

In some countries, private arrangements may be made between influential boards of trustees or parent associations at private international schools and the universities or ministries of the host country. Graduates of the American School of Vienna, whatever their nationality, are accepted at the University of Vienna. ("Do you know what you have to be to be admitted at the University of Vienna?" said Gordon Parsons while principal of this school. "Eighteen years old.") The American School of Brussels can send its "B" or better students to the University of Brussels (a private institution) in non-science faculties which do not require Latin. "I know the *recteur* pretty well," the Englishman Arthur Denyer said while head of this school, "and this was done over a dinner table, quite frankly, a few years ago." The American International School of Frankfurt receives a subvention from the State of Hesse, and its graduates are admitted at the University of Frankfurt — a concession which in principle extends also to German graduates, though in practice nobody has yet tried it. The American School of Madrid has made arrangements by which its graduates are taken at the University of Madrid with nothing more than an American high school diploma, and on the basis of this assurance has started moving Spanish students through the secondary grades. The program at the American School of Mexico City has been specifically approved, for students of all nationalities, by the Autonomous National University of Mexico. In Berlin the John F. Kennedy School is financed by the city government as a bilingual, U. S.-German joint venture, and its secondary program when completed will unquestionably be accepted by the Free University of Berlin, if not necessarily by the states of West Germany. Two Swedish private schools have been authorized to award a *Studentexamen* certificate for English-language programs similar but not identical to the Swedish program.

Cleverness in handling individual cases can often achieve results for which no routine procedure exists. The English-speaking International School of Milan, for example, has never been recognized by the University of Milan; and the British G.C.E. examinations for which it prepares are not recognized by the Italian universities as acceptable credentials for Italian nationals. Nevertheless, when the American Lionel Hoffman was headmaster of the school he found a way to beat a passage from his school to the university two miles away. He made arrangements with London University to admit as foreign students two of his Italians who had done well on G.C.E. A-levels. Then he got in touch with the Italian Ambassador in London, whose office investigated and certified to the University of Milan that these two Italians had in fact been admitted to the University of London. On the basis of their acceptance by London, they were admitted in their own home town, which they had never left.

Similarly, a Finnish girl studying at the American School of Brussels was informed that the diploma she was about to receive would not admit her to Helsinki. Denyer arranged her admission to the University of Brussels; the Finnish Ambassador to Belgium certified to Helsinki that the young lady had been accepted at Brussels; and thereupon she was accepted also by Helsinki. Sometimes it is possible to get eyes to blink at just the right moment. In one recent year, two Latin Americans at the American Catholic boarding school in Fribourg were accepted in their home universities on the basis of a certificate from the canton that they had completed the program of a "recognized school." Brother Moran, head of the school, told a visitor, "The certificate didn't say they could be admitted to the University of Fribourg, because they couldn't be. I don't know how it worked. Of course, they were the sons of the Mexican and Peruvian ambassadors."

Jan Van Der Valk of The Hague won admission to Dutch universities not only for a Turkish girl but also for a Dutch boy who had been through the American side of his international school. He said their admission "is not the kind of thing that can be done on principle — it is the kind of thing that you arrange with your friends." Nevertheless, Van Der Valk had shepherded both students through G.C.E. A-level in addition to their American diploma.

There is obviously a limit to how many such maneuvers can be executed. And most of the American overseas schools prepare only for American examinations and have been unable to make local arrangements of any sort. The Lincoln American School of Buenos Aires, for example, is half Argentinian in the elementary grades, but nude of Argentinians in the high school. From most American overseas schools, graduates can go only to the United States or to such American establishments abroad as Robert College in Istanbul or the American University of Beirut or the American College of Paris. For a European student, such options are almost worthless.

Atlantic College, built by Britons with the enthusiastic support of NATO headquarters and some financial help from

Access to Universities

the Ford Foundation, has hammered out what are in effect a series of private treaties between itself and a number of European universities and governments (not including the French). By the terms of these treaties, students from the signatory countries can come to Atlantic College for the last two years of their secondary program, and gain admission to their home universities on the basis of the British papers. On its side, Atlantic College has contracted to give each national group a number of hours every month in its own language, concentrating on history, civics and art.

Such arrangements, however, are inherently unstable. They depend upon year-to-year approval of the individual school by various national authorities which at best have other things to do with their time. Moreover, they are mildly distasteful to the sending countries, which agree to permit their nationals to be bound by the examination requirements of another nation — in this case, Great Britain. From the point of view of the school, moreover, they mock the internationalism of the effort by tying what is taught to one country's examination syllabus. There is a door at the end of the passage, in that the independent British examining syndicates can by their charters approve syllabi submitted to them by individual schools, and then prepare separate examinations to those syllabi, which will be equivalent to the ordinary examinations. But the more extensive the favors granted by the examinations syndicate, the more doubtful foreign governments will be about accepting the certificates for university entrance purposes at home.

5

Ultimately, if multinational secondary schools are to flourish, a way must be found to produce a single certificate universally acceptable as the equal of their own secondary certificates and basic university requirements by all the nations which send children to these schools. The model must be the sort of binational treaty which the French Ministry of Foreign Affairs negotiates on behalf of its overseas lycées, with the terms of reference made multinational. And the negotiations must be on behalf of the examination itself, not on behalf of individual private schools.

There are two existence theorems to prove the possibility. The older of them, representing little more than general acceptance of the *baccalauréat*, supported the NATO schools in France. Under the terms of the agreement, all the NATO nations accepted for university entrance the *baccalauréat* awarded by these two schools both to foreign students and to the local residents who made up about half the school population. The work of the foreigners was supplemented by six hours a week of instruction in their own languages by teachers supplied through agencies of their own governments. Though the United States and Britain could not officially commit universities to such arrangements, the admitting authorities in both countries felt obligations sufficiently considerable that graduates of these lycées regularly entered high-prestige American colleges with College Board scores well below the average of the domestic freshman class. These NATO schools have now been closed by the action of the French government expelling the headquarters of the organization from France; and at this writing it appears that at least one of the substitute schools formed in Belgium will be English-speaking.

More stable, because of the peaceful interests involved, is the treaty establishing the European Baccalaureate, signed in Luxembourg by representatives of the six Common Market countries on July 15, 1957. By the terms of this "Charter,"

Access to Universities

the European schools all teach the same program in the four languages of the Community, and the examinations are about the same for each language group (except, of course, for the native-language-and-literature component). For reasons to be noted in a later chapter, this arrangement has had its uneasy aspects; but the treaty has made it possible for international staffs to be working on identical material with a multinational group of children. The examination results are recognized by law in the six countries as equivalent to the parallel home certificates (with the single exception that the French will not accept the European Baccalaureate as sufficient for entrance to the preparatory classes for the *Grandes Ecoles*, which outrank the universities in the minds of many upper-middle-class Frenchmen); and the governments of Austria and Switzerland have also accepted the European certificate as valid for their own nationals. Though preference is given first to employees of the supranational European institutions and second to other citizens of the Common Market countries, about ten per cent of the students are of other nationalities, two to five per cent from the United States.

Political, technical and educational barriers stand in the way of creating similar privileges for less favored schools; these barriers will be examined in detail in Chapter 8. First it is necessary to look at some of the schools which would be involved, and the kinds and qualities of education they now offer to the children of the world's expatriate communities.

PART TWO

THE SCHOOLS

CHAPTER 3: **Ecolint, UNIS and Atlantic College: The Sponsors of the Examination**

The Athenians planted what passed for schools throughout the Mediterranean region hundreds of years before the birth of Christ, and the Genoese were educating their children at Pera across the Golden Horn from Constantinople in the middle of the medieval era. Mission schools came with the missionaries all over Africa and Asia during the heyday of imperialism, and some existing foreign secular schools — like the Lincoln American School of Buenos Aires and the Galatasary Lisesi of Istanbul — can trace their origins back into the nineteenth century. But the notion of *international* education is only a little more than forty years old, a product of the same burst of idealism and poor information about climate which set the League of Nations at the western end of Lac Léman in Calvin's Geneva.

But the idealism was real, and Geneva — a crossroads since Roman times, the fortress center of embattled international Protestantism and from the nineteenth century the home of the Red Cross, the first wholly international secular organization — was a suitable place for its out-of-town tryouts. Unlike the founders of compound schools for the children of diplomats or the entrepreneurs who made correspondence courses the foundation of boarding schools, the men who started the International School of Geneva in 1924 were not dominated by a felt need for instruction in a language other than that of the locality. They were engaged in building a new world for a human spirit freed from merely national constraints, and they wanted a school where their children could grow up as part of that new world. Though they wanted more teaching in English than the Swiss schools could offer, they were willing to operate mostly in French, which was the prime international language and was also, after all, the language children would find most useful while living in Geneva.

As a practical matter, the little group of civil servants and diplomats who were plotting the new school in early 1924 did want one American teacher; and among those making the plans was Arthur Sweetser, an American ex-newspaperman employed at the League of Nations, who was going back home for a visit. "They said," Sweetser recalled many years later from his retirement in Washington, " 'you find us a U. S. teacher, send her over, all expenses paid, salary paid, free to us. That's your job.'

"My wife," Sweetser continued, "knew the McCormicks — all these Chicago families are interrelated. And one of the McCormick ladies, an idealist, supported schools. She said she'd be delighted to pay the costs, and I wrote Geneva to say there was an American teacher on the way. They wrote back saying they'd lost their nerve and were going to wait until the next year. But I cabled: 'No, you've got to start some time.' "

Ecolint, UNIS and Atlantic College

The International School of Geneva opened in the autumn of 1924 with eight pupils and three teachers (one of them the American, the others Swiss), housed in a chalet loaned by a local supporter. By the end of the first year there were 29 pupils. When the doors opened in the autumn of 1925 there were 59. The villa was now overcrowded, and the school moved to a suite of apartments downtown.

"We then realized," Sweetser recalled, "that you can't make a go of a day school — you must have boarders to make the money. We took a villa in Onex, opened with one boarder, quickly went to ten and soon filled up. Then one of those crazy Americans came, said you need a girls' dorm — in town — got one for us — and we filled that up. We had classrooms on the Avenue Charles Bonnet, a house in the country, a house in town, and bus service."

At the end of the 1920s, with financial help from John D. Rockefeller, Jr., the Ecole Internationale de Genève bought out a business school at La Grande-Boissière, about a mile from the Geneva business district. The five buildings were more than enough for Ecolint, both physically and financially. Boarding quarters, classrooms and playing fields could easily be fitted into the establishment. Under the leadership of Mme Thérèse Maurette (whose father, Paul Dupuy, was secretary of the Ecole Normale Supérieure in Paris and a key personage in French education), Ecolint in the 1930s was a triumphant experiment, a source of psychological satisfaction for the community of the League and of intellectual accomplishment for their children. Financial insecurity, however, persisted, and there was still a large debt outstanding when World War II broke out and the international organizations closed down.

"We thought the war would kill us off," Sweetser said, "but we'd forgotten about the East European refugees, some of whom had some money and needed a school for their children. They kept us going. But we couldn't pay interest or amortization on the property. I went to the president of the Swiss Republic and I said, 'We think the canton ought to take it over for the outstanding obligations, and give us a twenty-year lease at a minimum sum. Otherwise we'll go into bankruptcy and you'll have to take over the education of all those children.' To my surprise, he agreed entirely."

Coming out of the war, then, Ecolint was a private school mostly on land leased from and in buildings maintained by the canton of Geneva. By a complicated formula, the school itself paid the maintenance on the dormitory facilities. Most of the staff was Swiss, paid (as is usual in private schools) slightly less than what Swiss teachers received in the state system. The expectation was that the school would resume its previous function as a special facility for the international civil servants, who would surely return at least to the International Labor Office, and eventually — though the new United Nations Organization was not to have its headquarters in Geneva — to the dreary pile of the Palais des Nations by the lake.

What had not been anticipated was the enormous increase in the presence and influence of the English-speaking community, and the great pressure on university entrance that came with economic reconstruction throughout the Western world. Before the war, Ecolint could see itself not merely as a service institution but also as the inventor of a truly international education for a relatively small number of students (at no time before 1939 were there more than 200 pupils in the school), most of them the children of either permanent expatriates or long-term residents of Geneva. The basic language of instruction was French, but everybody did some work in English, and there was special assistance to English-speaking students in the years just before university entrance, which was, in one way or another, nearly automatic in those days for all students who wanted it.

By 1950, Ecolint had 426 students, and there were two entirely separate streams in the school, one studying in French with English as a foreign language, the other in English with French as a foreign language. A single head, a single staff association and some shared athletic events and meals were the links between the "sides." But at least the sides were equal: 216 were in the English part of the school, 210 in the French part.

Then there came the rash of American businesses and banks, of short-term technical assistance specialists and supervisors for the World Health Organization and the International Labor Office, and for the European division of the United Nations. By 1967, there were almost 1,500 children at the school (still housed almost entirely at La Grande-Boissière, with the first and second grades sloughed off to an annex on the grounds of a Swiss secondary school half a mile away). Only a quarter of the students came from families where anybody worked at one of the international organizations — governmental or non-governmental. Half were Americans; only 367 (and a quarter of those English-speaking at home) were on the French side of the school. The boarding section was down to a few dozen children in outside rented villas, and no new boarders were being accepted. The demand for places at an English-speaking school in Geneva was so great that two rivals — a Lycée des Nations in town and a Collège du Léman just outside the city — were rapidly growing to uneconomic size with a flood of American day students. Though there remains a cadre of relatively permanent students at Ecolint, the average length of stay is now about two years.

The expansion was staffed from Britain. Though United

Kingdom students make up only 15% of the English side, United Kingdom teachers make up 76% of the faculty. The low salary scales for teachers in Britain in the 1950s made it relatively easy to recruit even at salaries which were then below $2,500 and were still below $5,000 in 1967, even for experienced teachers. The Swiss government was generous with permits to live and work in Switzerland, and with tax exemptions for foreign residents. Disparities in size, wealth and attitude broke apart the two sides of the school to the point where the institution functioned as a unit only through its single board of directors, its annual general assembly of parents and teachers and its once-a-year Student United Nations project. On the day-to-day basis from 1960 to 1967 there were separate directors for the two sides, separate staff associations, separate student organizations.

Physical facilities which were lavish before the war for 200 students are inevitably something less than adequate for 1,500, even after the conversion of former dormitory rooms to classrooms. It has been possible to borrow money to build a suite of six new science laboratories and about a dozen classrooms for the intermediate grades, but the school still lacks an auditorium, an indoor gymnasium, a reasonably adequate library and a place for instruction in music. Most students must go home or out for lunch because the dining facilities are altogether inadequate.

Ecolint is the largest and intellectually among the strongest of the "international schools." It has been a mother hen to the international schools movement, supporting with ideas and personnel several struggling ventures in multinational education in Africa, the eastern Mediterranean and Asia. The International Schools Association, with about two dozen members, had its headquarters on the school's property, and the attempt to write an international university entrance examination had its origins and its first secretariat here. Unlike most international schools, Geneva can show a relatively stable teaching group (less than ten per cent turnover in an average year). Moreover, though a number of the Swiss teachers on the French side are not fully trained (or licensed) and the foreign-language teaching staff on both sides seems to have been acquired *ad hoc*, the faculty is strong, especially in mathematics, science and history. Loyal alumni are scattered throughout the world, some of them in positions of considerable importance.

It is some measure of the problems that the international schools face, then, that the very survival of Ecolint was called into question during the mid-1960s. The root problem is financial. Bad accounting practice, loose control over the expenditure of funds and some unwise decisions (among them, the abandonment of the profitable boarding department) have aggravated the normal difficulties of making ends meet at a private school in a time of rapidly rising teacher salaries. In 1966–67, despite a fee increase to about $850 a child and contributions from several American businesses and the World Health Organization budget — and despite a large gift from a single private donor — Ecolint had to borrow money at the banks to carry its operating expenses.

Meanwhile, the new xenophobia of the Swiss has deprived the teachers of most of their former tax exemption and has made it increasingly difficult for the school to secure residence and work permits for its staff. (In 1965, an initiative to prohibit any further expansion of the international organizations carried the city of Geneva despite opposition by all political parties; it was kept off the statute books only by the votes of tolerant farmers in the outlying towns of the canton.) Renewal of the lease on La Grande-Boissière, which expires in 1968, will unquestionably involve the school in further expenses. All these problems are to be solved, it is said — and the physical limitations of the school plant are to be remedied — by the fund-raising work of a development committee, which talks in terms of tens of millions of dollars but in four years of solicitation has raised only a few tens of thousands.

In fact, the resources Ecolint needs are available only in America, and this is hard on a school which keeps at the heart of its self-image the fact that it is not an American school. Substantial efforts at fund-raising in America would certainly require a much better adjustment to the American parent body than the school has yet been able to manage. Robert Leach and Michael Knight of Ecolint have praised the Ghana International School at Accra for resisting the efforts of "the American patronage" to place it under "parent ownership and management, which has unfortunately proved the rock upon which more than one international school has foundered."[1] Contempt for American procedures, however, is a poor way to lure American contributions — especially when the only alternative visible to the staff has been the creation of an English school which is somehow not English. There then arises the difficulty that a school which the English see as "international" because it is somehow not English does not necessarily meet other people's definitions of internationalism.

Cruelly but not unfairly, it may be said that internationalism in Geneva in the 1960s was not carried beyond the point where it began to inconvenience the staff. On the English side there were no reception classes for students who came without English: the attitude was one of sink or swim. Those who needed assistance in English to keep up with their classes were encouraged to purchase private tutoring from the teach-

---

[1] "International Secondary Schools," Chapter II in George Z. Bereday and Joseph A. Lauwerys, eds., *The Year Book of Education, 1964*, Harcourt, Brace & World, New York, p. 450.

ers at the school. Teachers took no responsibility whatever for children outside the classroom: the school itself ran no bus service, and offered no supervision of the children before or after school or at tea time.

On the French side, to the annoyance of staff and board, the pretense that all the world knew the language of instruction could not be maintained in the face of a student body most of which did not speak French at home; and in the elementary division special classes were established for children whose French was weak. But these were not "reception" classes, from which it could be expected that children would advance to join the regular classes; they were simply inferior versions of the normal French-speaking class, formed partly in the hope that those slotted in this lower category would abandon the effort and (if their native language was English) shift over to the English side. For a time, no parent was more a figure of fun at the school than the American who wished to capitalize on a tour of duty in a French-speaking country by placing his child in a French-speaking school.

For all the influence which the French and English sides exerted on each other in the mid-1960s, one could have been in England and the other in France. From an early point in secondary school, the emphasis was on national examinations. On the French side, those who were not natively French-speaking were directed toward the Swiss program because, in the words of Jean Meyer, director of the French section, "It is almost impossible for those who do not speak French as a native language to pass the *baccalauréat*, not quite so impossible for them to pass the *maturité*." Students on the English side studied their French in books printed in England and aimed at English examinations; students on the French side studied their English in *Passport to English*, the French-edited and published series approved for the *baccalauréat*, in which the English are a strange people indeed. Despite the dominance of the English language at the school, French-speaking children were no more fluent in English at Ecolint than they were in the neighboring Swiss lycées. "The English-speaking stream of this school," said Nan Martin, a Scotch lady, married to a Swiss and teaching upper-level English on the French side, "may miss the advantages of living in a French-speaking city; but my kids have totally missed any advantage of being in an English-speaking school." It was almost unknown for a teacher from one side to visit classes on the other side to see how things were done; the staffs spent their tea times in different lounges and very rarely met together for any purpose. Relations between the two sides were inevitably exacerbated in times of financial stringency by the fact that the French side (with average classes of 10 or 12) was much more expensive to run than the English side (with average classes of 20 to 25).

What held this school together through the mid-1960s was its inescapable dependence on the Americans for students and money, on the British for low-priced staff, and on the Swiss for subsidy in the form of grounds and maintenance and for hospitality. Many members of the school community grew increasingly unhappy about the absence of significantly international work (as distinguished from international talk) at the school. The project for an international university entrance examination started at Ecolint not only because its practical necessity was obvious there (the necessity is equally obvious elsewhere) but even more because a handful of committed internationalists on the staff felt so strong a need to find something on which the French side and the English side could work together.

After a series of explosive confrontations in the spring of 1966, when the English-speaking side persuaded the school's

Ecolint, UNIS and Atlantic College

board to cut expenses by reducing French-speaking staff and French course offerings and then the French-speaking side persuaded the board to rescind the action, a mostly Swiss group committed to the continuance of the school moved in on the situation and changed the terms of reference. In the summer of 1967, a new board appointed a single director-general for the school as a whole — and he was an American, Irving Berenson of New York University. Having been director of broadcasting for the United Nations in Geneva for five years, Berenson was totally bilingual and generally sympathetic with the problems of the French side. He also enjoyed a fine, toughminded belief in efficiency as an independent value. With the support of his board, he spent the first months looking for ways to rationalize the employment of both space and staff at Ecolint; and to the staff itself he posed the question nobody had asked in a long, long time: "What is it that makes the education we offer here in any way *international* education?" Politically handicapped in every conceivable way — and with no experience in running a school (though he had taught in New York City high schools as a young man and had run a university department) — Berenson in late 1967, in the opinion of sympathetic members of the staff, looked to have a much better chance of making it than anyone would have given him at the moment of his arrival in September. In February of 1968, quite suddenly, he died, and the management of the school's problems was returned to its board.

FROM THE CLASSROOM

At the International School of Geneva, a class of about twenty 13–14-year-olds is studying English under the direction of Mme Nancy Poirel, a veteran of Ecolint, head of the secondary school on the English side. They are reading in a slim book of essays, and they had left off yesterday in a discussion of an essay about Hans Christian Andersen.

"The word the author used was *redemption*," Mme Poirel says. "Now, what did the author mean by that word? What do you think, Manda?" This doesn't wash, with Manda or anyone else; and Mme Poirel tries once more: "What is it that has saved these awful characters?" Still no luck. Rather than fuss over it, Mme Poirel reads a sentence from the essay about the characters being redeemed by the love of others. She moves on to the question of the role of *objects* in the Andersen stories, and now the children respond well with the observation that Andersen makes people out of objects. Mme Poirel moves to the new day's essay, which is a description of a fishing village.

"What did you understand by 'every ship is bound for Thule?' You may never have heard it before."

A boy says, "It's some place of fantasy."

"You're on the way."

Another boy says, "Like Disneyland."

"No," says Mme Poirel. "Not like Disneyland."

"Small islands," a girl ventures, "far away."

"Yes, far away." Mme Poirel tells them of the Greek traveler's story of having reached the final place. "The point is that he is saying every ship is setting off for a place the sailors don't really know exists." Then she asks their views on the description of one of the fishermen setting down the hill for the boats.

"It's kind of old-fashioned," a boy says, "like you read in most stories."

Another boy offers, "I think he describes him more or less like a story, not like the fishermen I've seen."

Mme Poirel asks, "Where do you see the striking difference between this fisherman and the fishermen you've seen?"

"Well," says the boy, "in South America they hardly wear any clothes at all."

"I think it's the boots," says a girl.

"I think so, too," says Mme Poirel. "You don't see boots that strike sparks from the cobbles, or boots that take the shape of people's legs. Have you ever run into these old leather boots with wooden soles and a strip of metal underneath? And what are cobbled streets? . . .

". . . What value does he have with the words 'all the boats are dancing' — rather than the synonyms you've proposed, *rocking, bouncing, swaying?*"

This is not a very bright class, but she holds them: an English teacher married to a Frenchman can convey in English the values of an *explication de texte*.

*   *   *

On the other side of the school, Mirian Weber is delivering to a group of eight children the same age a lesson in French. He says, "Of the great authors after Molière, we study especially Marivaux." Notebooks are out and pens are writing busily. "The eighteenth century was brilliant in Paris, the topic of the light theatre was love. . . . Marivaux must be seen as part of a line from Thibaud de Champagne in the twelve hundreds to Giraudoux today. . . . In studying *Le Jeu de l'Amour et du Hasard* we must see especially the *perspective* of the comedy. . . . It is very difficult for today's actors to recover the motions, the *alertness* of the actors of that time. Now, what is the use of these metaphors? . . . Racine also analyzed love, but came out always with catastrophe. . . ."

*   *   *

Alfred Rocquet, for several years head of the French side of the school and now semi-retired to a part-time teaching schedule, is taking a group of ten boys and girls in the last year of the French program through a lesson in geography. One of the boys distributes to the students a set of magnificent atlases, theirs for the class period only. Rocquet explains to the visitor that each of the students was assigned a country on which to report, but the boy who was to report today is sick, so Rocquet will improvise a lesson.

He chooses the Danube basin, reviews the terms of the Versailles Treaty in dismantling the Austro-Hungarian Empire and stripping Hungary of Transylvania and Ruthenia, mentions the main mountain chains (and the very different ways of spelling them in French and English), discusses the Danube lakes (like Lac Léman, which is part of the Rhone), informs the class that the Danube carries more tonnage than the Rhone, which is today only the fourth shipping artery of Europe, discusses the international treaty governing navigation on the river, brings up the two dangerous passages (in the plains, where sand bars form, and at the Gate of Fire between the Transylvanian Alps and the Balkan Mountains), describes the channels to the Rhine at the western end and the channels cut to the Black Sea at the eastern end (necessary because the descent is so slow and the river tends to form separate streams, leaving islands where the gypsies live), tells of the Rumanian Black Sea resort of Mamaia and the Rumanian effort to draw tourists, the cheap boat trip down the river from Vienna.

Then he goes to the riparian countries, especially Hungary: the valley of the Tisza, where Tokay comes from, and its two tributaries, the Carosse and the Marosse; the climate (very continental, with extremes from –30°C. to +45°C.); the fact that Hungary, Transylvania and the Ukraine are the granaries of Europe — "But where does Switzerland get her wheat? From Canada, the United States and the Argentine. The Swiss government has been trying to get wheat grown in Switzerland, and will pay a premium, but the farmers are not interested...."

*   *   *

On the English side a group of 15–16-year-olds studies O-level geography with Philip Thomas, a cheerful young Welshman who enjoys baffling polyglot Geneva by speaking Welsh in restaurants with another member of the social studies department. There are 26 children in this class. Today's lesson is on trees. Thomas summons students to the board to make a diagram of the economic uses of trees: the extracts (from syrup and rubber to chicle); the bark (cork, quinine, etc.); timber; fruit. He refers the class to the textbook and says, "You can spend the next five minutes writing down in your notes the value of tree products in world trade." While the children write he comes to talk with the visitor.

"For O-level," he explains, "they must prepare two regions, plus general geography, and a survey of world trade. We're going to deal with rubber. In the exam the examiner often asks them to reproduce a sketch map of one area...."

He returns to the head of the room and says to the class, "All right, let's come back then and concentrate our attention on rubber. Macintosh made the first waterproof fabric for raincoats. He married a French girl from Clermont-Ferrand. Goodyear invented vulcanization, Dunlop invented the pneumatic tire." He writes on the board, *Hevea brasiliensis*. "In the tropical forest," he explains, "there's a great variety of trees, and species are not grouped together...."

* * *

A group of 16-year-olds on the English side are working on the international history syllabus developed by Ecolint in the early stages of work toward an international examination, and their leader is its author, Robert Leach, chairman of the department, an American Quaker who is a permanent resident of Geneva. This course, called "inner and outer," devotes more than usual attention to the history of what is now the Third World. A boy is reporting on developments in China and Japan in the twelfth century, reading from notes he has taken on an encyclopedia article. He gives the division of China, Genghis Khan, the Fujiwara family in Japan and the creation of the shogunate.

"Yesterday," Leach says, "we had a little discussion of the change of dynasties in Korea, and the division of north, central and southern India. Now, why are we doing this outside area from 925 to 1200?"

A girl, called upon for a reply, says, "Well, there's going to be a question on it on the exam."

"Yes, yes," says Leach. "That's a very practical reason." Nobody can supply another, so he moves on to the expansion of the Arabs after 1100, the Murabit Empire, the Empire of Mali, the conquest of the Christian kingdom of Nubia.

2

The establishment most closely related to Ecolint in situation and purposes is the United Nations International School in New York City. Started in 1947 as a nursery school in the Guest House of the U. N. Secretariat, which was then in the suburbs at Lake Success, UNIS became a full-scale diploma-granting institution only in 1962. Its offerings on the secondary level have been limited by the existence of a well-established private French lycée in New York and by the willingness of most of the large Asian, African and South American contingents to send their children to American colleges. At great expense, however, the school has consistently offered General Certificate of Education programs to the few students destined for British universities.

Like the Geneva school, UNIS has benefited by the stability of the international secretariats, which together with the natives provide a fairly large semi-permanent student cadre: the average stay at the school is about four years. Teachers, however, tend to be less permanent, because the American government grants only a two-year exemption from income taxes, and because the apparently high salaries at the school (up to $8,500) shrink in value when the teachers confront the costs of middle-class existence in New York. In 1967, the French and American governments concluded an unpublicized deal by which each nation's teachers resident in the other's territory would be excused from income taxes for the duration of their employment; repercussions on the UNIS staff were horrendous.

Although a private school with high fees (up to $1,250 in the secondary division), UNIS is the beneficiary of an annual "grant-in-aid" from the General Assembly to make up its deficit. In bad years, this grant has approached $100,000. The school has also been attractive to the Ford Foundation, which has pledged $7.5 million (and conceivably more) to the construction of a home for the institution. Up to 1967, the school was abominably housed; part of its elementary division was in a group of apartments in Parkway Village, a middle-income housing development in the Borough of Queens, and much of the elementary division and the secondary division in an abandoned New York City elementary school built in the 1890s. During the 1967–68 academic year, UNIS moved to a converted loft-showroom building near the East River, which will serve as a temporary home until arrangements can be made for something more permanent. Both staff and parents have been repeatedly frustrated by the inability of the school's board (dominated by the Secretariat) to settle on a site for a new building.

About one-third of the 700-odd UNIS students are New Yorkers, about two-fifths are from the Secretariat, seven or eight per cent come from the delegations to the United Nations, and the rest are the children of non-U. S. businessmen, professors, etc., working in the New York area. The plans for new buildings have called for a school of 1,500 (funds permitting).

At this writing, a French-language elementary school is part of the establishment in Parkway Village, and schedules are coordinated to make sure the French-speaking and English-speaking children spend part of each day together. This makeshift is to be phased out at some point (with the full consent of the French government authorities in New York); and the entire school is to be made bilingual, offering most academic work in English but some (other than the language itself) in French. The school also hopes to offer each national group six hours a week in its own language, with courses in its own history and culture and current home developments. This approach is condemned in Geneva — and, therefore, automatically, by the International Schools Association — as a source of national divisions, which presumably would not otherwise exist. But it is probably over the long run a requisite if the various government educational authorities are to grant full recognition to the work of an international school; and it offers to many children (especially to those whose native language is neither English nor French) an invaluable psychological support. At present the school provides — after hours but without charge — language and literature instruction in Arabic, Chinese, Hebrew, Hindi, Russian, Spanish and Urdu.

The headmaster of the school during its developmental period was Ulf Østergaard, a coolly intelligent Dane who had come to international work almost accidentally, through attendance at a UNESCO meeting in 1947. There he met a Philippine senior civil servant who later got him seconded by the Danish authorities for work in Manila as an educational adviser. (International education seems to get into the blood: safely returned to Denmark and director of one of Copenhagen's newest and best secondary schools, Østergaard has become sponsor and nursemaid to a new international school, with Danish governmental recognition and support, planned for his home city.) On Østergaard's departure, the board of the school took the New Zealander Aleck Forbes from Ecolint; and when Forbes left in 1964 UNIS reached down to Rio for the gentle Englishman Desmond Cole, who had built the American school of that city into one of the most attractive and ambitious in the world.

"We are," Cole has written in the UNIS handbook for teachers, "a team rather than a hierarchy." Appropriately, UNIS has the most international staff in the world, with the British accounting for about a quarter, and the British–American–white Commonwealth nations for only about a half. After much travail — and long negotiations to assure Cole at least in principle the right to choose the individual himself — the Polish and Russian governments have agreed to second one teacher each; and Cole's second-in-command, Maurice Pezet, is in effect seconded by the French government, though his salary is paid entirely by UNIS. Staff meetings are frequent (some teachers think too frequent); moreover, especially in working with that 40% to 50% of the children whose native language is not English, the teachers are expected to give considerable attention to individual problems.

By and large, language teachers at UNIS are native speakers of the language. History and geography teachers tend to be British or American; and there is always at least one mathematics teacher from Denmark. Most science courses are based on the American "reform" programs — P.S.S.C. physics, B.S.C.S. biology, Chem Study chemistry, developed under leadership from the universities with some tens of millions of dollars of tax money assigned by the National Science Foundation — though G.C.E. syllabi must of course be followed in the G.C.E. courses. The science department is also developing, under grant from Ford, an original "sociology of science" course.

Academically, the school is extremely ambitious. Its official objective at the opening of the secondary program was, in the words of an early fund-raising brochure, "to bring the student to the level of proficiency that would be required for his age by the most exacting school system to which he might transfer. Thus, if one national system places a priority on early mathematical skill while another emphasizes skill in composition, the standard adopted by the United Nations School would be the most advanced in each subject." Cole, who is perhaps a more practical schoolman than his predecessors, has accepted this policy but modified it in his teachers' manual with the comment that "academic standards . . . are set as high as it is believed possible to achieve at each stage." Moreover, the school hopes that, except in the courses directed toward specific examinations, every teacher will accept an obligation to be international in his approach — a commitment, as the teachers' handbook puts it, "to know what of significance is being done in his field in other countries."

"One of the goals of the school," said the 1963 fund-raising brochure, "has been the establishment of a United Nations International School Diploma, which would be internationally recognized in lieu of other university or college entrance requirements." Fed by the optimism of some of the trustees from the Secretariat — whose attitude toward the school has often been that of the fight manager assuring a battered tiger that his opponent "hasn't laid a glove on you" — this objective was retained until 1965, when the entire graduating class of 19 (17 of them girls) were candidates for American colleges. The small terminal class, and the visible departure at an earlier age of those destined for university in other countries, forced Cole to a reconsideration of the school's chances of winning acceptance for its Diploma. As a result, UNIS joined Geneva and Atlantic College as a prime sponsor of the effort to create an international university entrance examination.

FROM
THE CLASSROOM

At the United Nations International School, in a small room once used as an office, Brian Kahn, a teacher from England, is experimenting with an anthropology course for seven children of mixed secondary ages. "Remember," he says, "the amino acid point. There's a correspondence in chemical composition of sixty per cent between man and the horse, ninety-five per cent between man and the primates. Chemically, we can't explain the transition between *Homo erectus* and *Homo sapiens.*" Lights dim and one of the boys begins to operate a slide projector. "These are the four periods of glaciation. The oldest evidence for man goes back prior to the first period. You'll remember that our only way of defining 'man' is as a primate who does culture...."

Other slides show results from the work of Leakey in the Olduvai Gorge in East Africa, *Homo habilis,* different sizes of brain case. "Now we have Carleton Coon and the theory of five separate evolutions. I think one should view this with considerable suspicion — it is implied that the Caucasoid race got there first, and I think any theory that produces this result should be viewed with suspicion. The great geneticist Dobzhansky opposes it because of the unlikelihood of five separate evolutions, the insistence that characteristics must be linked, and couldn't be inherited separately as they are in intermarriage...."

*   *   *

Chester Nimmons, a young Irishman with a casual manner who taught at Geneva before coming to the United Nations School, is carrying a class of 16 eleventh-graders (14 of them girls) through European history. He starts with the news:

"There was an explosion in Southern Ireland last night. Did you hear about it?"

"Yes."

"What was it about?"

"A girl says, "The fiftieth anniversary of the Revolution."

"Who did it?"

"Irish extremists," the girl replies.

"Why?"

They know the answer to that; and they also know that it is most unlikely that the Northern Irish want any part of the answer.

"Where is President Johnson today and why?" They know that one, too (it was the meeting at Punta del Este). "This is the date of President Lincoln's assassination. Who did it?" They know that. "What did a man named Payne have to do with it?" — and someone knows even that. "Good." Something less than five minutes have elapsed.

Nimmons bends to his notes. "This lesson is about the Reformation in the far North. The situation was dominated by the Union of Kalmar in 1397. As there are no adequate maps here I shall excel myself once more." Turning to the blackboard, he draws a very adequate map of Denmark, Norway, Sweden, and the western Baltic. "The Danish king ruled the three of them," he says to the blackboard, placing a dot for Kalmar in Sweden. "They were supposed to be irrevocably joined for foreign affairs. In 1520 the King of Denmark — Christian II, who had come to power in 1513 — crossed over the strait, marched into Sweden and arrived in Stockholm, where he defeated the Swedes easily. Christian executed eighty Swedish leaders in the public square. After that there was no more opposition and he went away, saying to himself, 'That was a good day's work.' But as in Ireland, this had what result?"

One of the girls says, "The Swedes kept fighting."

"Yes," says Nimmons. "Like the Belgians when Alba tried it. The Swedes found another leader, very famous, Gustavus Vasa. In 1523 he was elected King of Sweden."

One of the boys breaks in: "Elected by whom?"

"Elected by the Swedes," Nimmons continues rather smoothly, "King of Sweden. And during the next two hundred years, Sweden, strangely enough, became one of the great powers of Europe."

He turns back to the map and puts an X on the southern shore of the Baltic. "There is a city here," he says. "Name begins with L. Anybody know it?"

Three or four voices call, "Lübeck."

Very impressive.

*   *   *

At Atlantic College, a class of eight boys (one each from the United States, Germany and Burma, two from Wales and three

Ecolint, UNIS and Atlantic College

from England) is working toward G.C.E. A-level physics, and reviewing a unit. "We've been talking," says the teacher, "about the types of radioactive decay observed in the early years of this century, and the problem of electric field versus magnetic field." He puts an equation on the board: "Which way is the electric field flowing? . . ." Another equation: "You've noticed that the atomic number does not change. Beta decay is quite common, alpha decay makes greater difference in the periodic table. . . . The apparatus that was in use about 1930 was cheap and easy to build in universities. But as the energies required became higher one had to bring industry into it." He draws a graph of uranium-235 en route to uranium-238: "This is a log scale, you'll remember, and this jagged point is the resonance push. We worked it out, and came to the conclusion that you're going to get ten to the twelfth joules of energy for every gram of uranium destroyed.

"U-238 goes to U-239 at high energies; then there's a beta decay to neptunium-239, another beta decay to plutonium-239. What do we call this sort of reaction?"

The American and an English boy react together: the American says "breeder" (which is correct); the English boy says "chain" (which is wrong). The teacher continues, "During the war the main purpose was to produce plutonium, and the great problem was getting rid of the heat. The heat was a waste. Now, in our peaceful applications, we want as much heat as we can handle. . . ."

3

Atlantic College, as its name hints, was conceived by the intellectual fringe of the essentially military North Atlantic Treaty Organization. Some people had been reading Kurt Hahn, the German educator whose "Outward Bound" philosophy of communion through shared physical effort and danger has automatic appeal to the military sensibility; others were acquainted with Gordonstoun, the British "public school" based on Hahn's work, which had prepared Prince Philip and was in process of training his son. From conversations about

Hahn came the idea of a school which would prepare for future high-level collaboration an elite of young men from all the nations of NATO, and in January 1962 a firm decision was made to open such an institution that September. Because much of the impetus toward founding such a school was British, the age group chosen was the last two years of secondary education, where the English Sixth Form, at least in theory, makes men from boys. But the two-year Atlantic College actually begun in Wales is seen not as an isolated enterprise but as the first of a chain of such schools, and the sponsoring group has been in negotiations since 1964 in Germany and Canada to create more. In each country, unless the drive for an international examination succeeds, the local Atlantic College will prepare students for the examination of its hosts; and the language will of course be that of the environment.

Few schools are so beautifully situated (or so remote) as the existing Atlantic College, which stands in a lavishly reconditioned castle on the north shore of the Bristol Channel. The channel provides the Outward Bound experiences: the boys are organized into rescue teams which prowl the waters or climb the cliffs. The channel is legitimately dangerous because of the rapid and immense (42-foot) rise and fall of the tide, which can easily strand vacationers and adventurous children, and not all the rescue alarms are false: three or four people may owe their lives to the training Atlantic College students have received. During the winter, water skills are practiced in a large outdoor swimming pool where the water is heated but the air is not.

At work Outward Bound, the boys wear rubber suits, and one group of them paddles the channel in kayaks that seal against the waist — wonderfully buoyant and maneuverable, but a bit of a problem when they tip, leaving heads underwater. The wives of the faculty are particularly terrified when such accidents occur a hundred yards out in the channel, with the

Ecolint, UNIS and Atlantic College

kayak sweeping in over reefs just below the surface; but nobody has been seriously hurt yet.

Atlantic College has about 200 students, all boys (though the staff would like to see coeducation), all living on the grounds, some in the castle itself and some in one-story wooden dormitories built on the manor a short muddy walk away. Roughly a third of the students are British — and of these a number are Scottish, who feel themselves, not unreasonably, as foreign as anyone else to the mysteries of English education. (The Scottish system is less specialized than the English on the upper secondary and university-entrance levels.) A sixth or so are Americans and about a tenth are from the white Commonwealth. Most of the rest are continental Europeans, with the German and Scandinavian contingent especially strong. The age range is 17 to 20, with most boys 18 or 19. Most Americans are at Atlantic College for one year; they have already finished high school, many of them know where they are going to college, and this international Sixth Form is essentially an exploratory year abroad.

Students are a mixture not only in terms of nationality but also in social class. There are no scholarships for Americans, whose parents are almost universally professional and executive. The British contingent, on the other hand, is recruited largely from the middle and lower-middle classes, from the city grammar schools rather than from the boarding "public schools." The Scandinavians and Germans are a mixed bag, many on scholarship provided by home-country sponsors (both Norway and Sweden have government-sponsored scholarships to Atlantic College), the rest from the *haute bourgeoisie*. Nearly all the Latins and Levantines are from that upper crust which is the only internationalist element in the area.

The normal obligations owed by a school to its students are greatly, even dangerously, intensified here. Nobody comes to Atlantic College as a matter of course or of necessity: the school must recruit. For continental Europeans, the school has sought agreement that G.C.E. A-level scores which would be good enough to win admission at a British university will be accepted for university entrance at home. By and large the boys who come to Atlantic College would be sure to succeed at their own national examinations — or at least the parents who send them think so. Thus, while Ecolint can function with an A-level failure rate ranging from 15% to 50%, Atlantic College must get everybody through.

Teachers who left secure positions at other schools to participate in this experiment are not prepared to see themselves as cogs in an examination-passing machine. The school itself has much more idealistic ends in view. There must be time for the Outward Bound derring-do and (by agreement with the education ministries of the sending nations) for instruction in native language and culture. The headmaster, Admiral Hoare, observed rather sourly, "We must offer two hours a week of Walloon history." Moreover, the school believes in both art and music, for the making of the whole man and for significant contact between the products of different national backgrounds.

While the ordinary British public school can give Sixth Form students nine periods (seven hours) a week in each of the three subjects they will carry through to A-level examinations, Atlantic College cannot manage more than seven periods (a little more than five hours). Some students are simply not capable of doing the very intense work required by A-level — especially in a language not their own. The wide choice of subjects offered by the examining syndicates at A-level helps in individual cases: a student who would be in serious trouble in mathematics or science or classics or English can scrape through with A-levels in his own language, art history and ceramics; but this record card may be touchy back home. Reality in the form of study strictly for examinations is forever breaking in on the students' enthusiasms.

Atlantic College, in short, fulfills a dream rather than a need. It is none the worse for that. The staff — young but experienced, highly competent, with that specially English combination of kindliness and bluntness — is far better than could have been recruited by any new private school trying to do what other private schools do. The more than two million dollars that has been raised from the British and German governments and the Ford and Nuffield foundations for physical facilities — all first-rate except the science laboratories, which are still housed in former stables and minimally equipped — would not have been available to a new private school which did not have the special attractions of Atlantic College. But there is inevitably a certain artificiality about the institution. Few of the boys take the rescue training seriously (though most of them like it), and when they talk about world affairs they speak of an unreal Earth which can be brought to Peace by the exercise of nothing more difficult than Goodwill. In the spring of 1965, a pre-arranged bull session of a dozen boys from England, America and the Continent were all agreed, beyond the possibility of doubt, that within a year or two the Common Market countries and the Outer Seven would achieve economic union and even a measure of political union: they were the advance guard themselves. And they had a Cold War sense of geography, lacking any notion that Prague and Budapest were no less "European" than Paris or Brussels. Just as the Fulbright program has brought to America as students those non-Americans most favorably inclined toward the United States, Atlantic College has recruited boys most of whom would be internationalist in attitude, in a Western way, if they never left home. The social role of Ecolint and UNIS is quite obvious; the function of Atlantic College is obscure.

But of the three schools pioneering in the effort to create an international examination, Atlantic College probably makes the greatest contribution. The number of its annual graduates destined for British or Continental universities is by far the largest and on balance the most likely to succeed, because neither Ecolint nor UNIS can select its students as Atlantic College can. University entrance is an all-day every-day concern of the entire staff and its leadership (and of all the students, one of whom remarked wistfully at the bull session that the Americans were the happiest group in the place because they already knew where they were going to college). Moreover, because all the Atlantic College students come directly from middle-secondary work in their own countries (rather than up the school's own ladder or from other international schools), the staff is forcibly confronted with the differences in what national systems do. Because Atlantic College has never hoped for a world where its "diploma" could replace results on external examinations as a means of entry to university, its teachers are better equipped to analyze the real gains from the convenience of an international program as against the real losses of freedom from the imposition of a compromise curriculum. At the meetings to plan an international examination, the Atlantic College teachers are almost always better informed and wiser than their colleagues from the other schools, though their orientation is often more English than they realize. (Part of the price the International Baccalaureate Office has had to pay for Atlantic College participation is adoption of the Nuffield Foundation unified physics-chemistry course and G.C.E. exam as part of an international program.) And the level of work at Atlantic College is sufficiently high that the leadership does not have to fear any demands which might be made by an international standard.

CHAPTER 4: **The Scholae Europaeae**

The six Scholae Europaeae of the Common Market can be seen as a monument to the persistence and ability of one man — Albert van Houtte, the burly, rather sarcastic *greffier* of the court of the European Coal and Steel Community, with headquarters in Luxembourg. "There are four international organizations here," he explained shortly before the French forced a rationalization of the Common Market secretariats, "each with a secretary-general. The other three secretaries-general decided that the secretary-general of the court did not have much to do, so he should start a school."

Van Houtte's own interest was in a school for his children. As the tenth-anniversary book of the Luxembourg Schola Europaea noted, the Grand Duchy was hospitable to foreigners and its French-German bilingualism was international in flavor (with a "*double ascendance à la culture latine et à la culture germanique*"[1]). Still, this kind of bilingualism was of lesser

[1] *Schola Europaea Luxembourgensis, 1953–1963*, p. 41.

value to the Italian and Dutch employees of the Community — and to the Flemish, like van Houtte. And some courses in the local schools were taught in the local dialect, which was not acceptable to anybody except the Luxembourgers.

At first, in the early 1950s, the Community organized bus service for children to nearby French, Belgian and German schools for the nationals of these countries; but it was offensive to the spirit of the new organization that the children of those brought together in service to the new Europe should be separated by educational requirements. The presidents of the four institutions based in Luxembourg (they were major European political figures — Paul-Henri Spaak, Jean Monnet, Michel Rasquin and Massimo Pilotti) considered the question and voted *not* to create an official school, but to give "moral and material" encouragement (including some budgetary support) to any group of employees who wished to start what would be a private school.

With van Houtte as president, the employees formed a non-profit corporation, the Association of Educational and Family Interests of non-Luxembourgian E.C.S.C. Functionaries, which was in turn granted by the government of the Grand Duchy a special charter to run a school. The school — kindergarten and five grades — opened in a battered private house on October 4, 1953, with six teachers, one from each of the countries in the Community, and 70 students (26 French, 16 German, 13 Dutch, 11 Belgians and 4 Italians). By the end of the first year there were 140 students; and every one of the 20 fifth-graders who went to Trier, Thionville and Arlon to qualify for secondary school in his own country passed the admissions test.

Meanwhile, van Houtte and his fellow functionaries had made a survey of their colleagues and uncovered about a hundred children of secondary age. Their parents were invited to a meeting which turned "passionate," demanding a European secondary school to match the elementary school. This demand was carried to a meeting of the Assembly of the Community in Strasbourg in the spring of 1954, and the delegates passed a motion calling upon the High Authority to make the necessary arrangements with the sponsoring governments. Rather reluctantly, René Mayer, president of the High Authority, sent out the letters. "He told me," van Houtte recently recalled, " 'You will never succeed. Make a good private school. You can have Adenauer and de Gasperi on your board of trustees, you will get privileged treatment.' But we needed more than privileged treatment."

By July 1954, less than a year after the opening of the original primary school, the chiefs of "middle" education or secondary education of all the six countries were meeting in Luxembourg with van Houtte and his committee to plan an acceptable secondary program. In two days the six agreed with the influential parents' association on the basic principles of a European school, and gave a go-ahead to the (still private) association to undertake the first two years of secondary education, with guaranteed transfer to the third year in the national systems. By December, this agreement had been ratified by all the participating ministries, and the group turned its attention to the much more difficult problem of the latter years of secondary school. On the motion of the French delegation, the group agreed to seek a European Baccalaureate which would be accepted by all six countries. Now the hard work began.

"We did a big table of the programs in the six countries," van Houtte recalled. "Everyone has his mother tongue, mathematics, a second language, physics, etcetera — there's a seventy per cent overlap. There remains the other thirty per cent." For three years representatives of the six ministries of education met periodically, in Luxembourg and elsewhere, to iron out the wrinkles in the thirty per cent. It was a labor which required, as the history of the Luxembourg school puts it, "a large opening of views together with a sharp sense of realities, because one cannot impose on students the addition pure and simple of the programs of each country."[1] Most of the meetings were discouraging, and in 1955 van Houtte went to the International Schools Association, the private-school group dominated by Geneva, to plead for their support of an international examination and their help in developing it. The plea was rejected: 1955 was the heyday of the attitude that Europe was dead and that the future belonged to the developing countries, an attitude much reinforced at I.S.A. by its hard-won third-category affiliation with UNESCO.

More than that: van Houtte came to I.S.A. as a spokesman for public education. Though his school was private, he was already demanding in the meetings with the inspectors-general and directors of the ministries that their governments pay the bills for the Schola Europaea in Luxembourg. "An international school," he said, "should not be a privilege for those able to pay for it, a ghetto of the rich. If I had been a member of the U. N. in New York or in Geneva, I would have fought to make these schools free." I.S.A. was committed to a contrary philosophy. As J. D. Cole-Baker put it when director of the English side at Ecolint, "An international school must be non-governmental; otherwise each goverment has the right to say what should be taught." Indeed, the rules for admission to I.S.A. were until 1966 so restrictive that any school which accepted financial help from any government was theoretically ineligible for membership.

[1] *Schola Europaea Luxembourgensis, 1953–1963*, p. 45.

The moment of possible collaboration passed, and van Houtte won his struggles by himself. It was a great achievement. "My signature as a German," says Karl Voss, head of the Luxembourg school, "is worth as much in France as the signature of the *proviseur* of a French lycée. You cannot know what a miracle that is."

The national ministries of education compromised on their thirty per cent disagreement, drew up a program and agreed on an examination which, translated into all four languages, would be the same for all. On April 12, 1957, an intergovernmental board took over from the parents' association the management and financing of the Schola Europaea of Luxembourg, and on the 15th of July representatives of the six countries signed the treaty establishing the European Baccalaureate. The Luxembourg government itself had already begun construction of a new building to house the school, and by December 1957 a lavishly appointed and typically French school building, blank walls with windows like boxes, was opened near the center of Luxembourg to house 800 students.

These were the years of the negotiation and signing of the Treaty of Rome and the development of Euratom. "The atmosphere was propitious then as it is not now," van Houtte said in 1965. "At present we could never succeed with such a venture." But the creation of the Common Market and of Euratom solidified the function of the Schola Europaea. At the insistence of Walter Hallstein, a parallel school was established for the European Economic Community's growing staff at Brussels; and then Etienne Hirsch of Euratom demanded the same privileges for the employees of his four research installations. By 1967 there were six schools, more than 400 teachers and nearly 6,000 students; both Brussels and Luxembourg were seriously crowded. Though the French have been grumbling about costs and the Dutch have been irritated by the way Netherlands history is taught, the system is now too firmly established to be threatened by any resurgent nationalism which is not strong enough to break up the European Economic Community itself.

The central principle of the Scholae Europaeae is that every child is entitled to an education in his own language. Thus each school is divided into four linguistic sections — French, German, Italian and Dutch-Flemish — and each child does most of his academic work in his mother tongue. From the first year of school, however, five hours every week are given to the study of a second language, which must be German for the French-speaking and French for the German-speaking but may be either French or German for the Italian- and Dutch-speaking. And 6½ hours every week are for "European subjects" — a term of art meaning music, art, physical education and shop — and free play, for all of which the linguistic groups are mixed. The school week runs 25½ hours in the first two grades, 29½ hours in the next three; the child takes 40% of his time at the beginning and more than a third later studying a second language or playing in multilingual groups. Instruction in the second language is given according to achievement groups — fifth-graders with no previous French will study French with second- and third-graders similarly situated, not with their own class.

The seven-year secondary school is divided into two parts: a three-year general preparatory period in which all students follow the same program, and a four-year second cycle permitting a degree of specialization in classical languages, math-science, math-science *sans* Latin, or economics and political science. (The last of these options is new and still unpopular.) Everyone studies Latin (*the* European language) at least in the second and third years; and from the third year to the conclusion of the school everyone must study English. These classes are not mixed: each linguistic group learns English by

The Scholae Europaeae

reference to its own "language of control." In the third year, 17 of 33 hours (21 of 37 hours for the French-speaking Belgians, who must also study Flemish) are given to the teaching of the mother tongue, Latin, and modern foreign languages. Music, art, physical education and shop continue to be "European subjects," with mixed groups. From the second year, students must do their work in history and geography in a "vehicular language" — French for the Germans, German for the French, one or the other for the Dutch and Italians.

The International Schools Association likes to speak of the Scholae Europaeae as really "four schools under one roof," and indeed the staffs are forever trying to think up ways that the different linguistic streams can be better mixed in the European subjects and in such extracurricular activities as student government, astronomy clubs and chess clubs, which tend to be dominated by the French and the French-speaking Belgians.

Different degrees of integration have been achieved in different schools. A French-language geography class visited at Varese in Italy consisted of three Italians, six Dutch, one Flemish-speaking Belgian, six Germans, four French whose German was not yet up to par and (in the fine precision of the French teacher) four absent — the absent have no nationality. On the other hand, a French-language history class visited at Brussels was composed entirely of students from the Italian section. In Brussels, despite the construction of a four-story blue glass–and–aluminum classroom building, many classes are still held in temporary wooden structures scattered over the eighteen acres of the old suburban Chateau Rhier, donated by the Belgian government for this purpose; in Varese and in Luxembourg, all classes are in wings of large main buildings.

In Luxembourg and in Varese (and doubtless in the three

other, much smaller schools affiliated with Euratom projects), students are always conscious that they are attending an international school. Classrooms are assigned to groups by age level only, so children of different nationalities are forever bumping into one another in the halls; and the student asked to describe the atmosphere of his school for the tenth-anniversary book of the Luxembourg school wrote that a newcomer's first reaction is always to wonder how he ever got mixed up in this Tower of Babel. The fact that everybody is following much the same program often means, too, that a student's notes or homework, or guesses at examination questions, may be highly relevant to the problems of another student from a different linguistic group. At least, there is at the Scholae Europaeae a sense of shared *problems*.

The teaching staffs especially share problems across linguistic lines, because all must teach roughly comparable programs for an identical examination. Teachers are not recruited by the schools; they are seconded by their national ministries. The director of an individual school may reject a teacher after a year, in theory from any country though in practice only from his own country. But there are very few teachers whom anyone would like to reject. Because the ministers of education are themselves the governing council of the Scholae Europaeae, the bureaucracies have all put their best foot forward. Salaries — which are not public information — are believed to be the highest in Europe. The teachers regard themselves as an elite corps, and they are. They can therefore cooperate on a basis of high mutual respect, and they do. At lunch, subject matter groups are as usual as nationality groups in the staff rooms, and teachers from different countries are forever meeting in the evenings in one another's homes to drink beer and lay plans to sabotage all the national bureaucracies.

That such sabotage is necessary is a matter of universal

agreement. Because the program for these schools was established by treaty, no changes can be made without treaty modifications requiring the acceptance of officialdom in all six countries. The program in mathematics established in 1957 was wildly out of date eight years later, but the ministries had been unable to agree on a new one. Thus first-rate teachers, who would be in the vanguard of reform movements in their own countries, were in theory compelled by the Schola Europaea inspectorate to teach in ways they had long since abandoned at home. At the Schola Europaea in Varese in 1965 the mathematics departments of the different sections joined to give two hours a week after school, on a voluntary basis, to students working in the math-science specialties, to bring them up to date on the reformed programs in their home countries.

By 1967, the success of the schools was measurable in university terms. Though the home schools grumbled (especially about the alleged incompetence of transfers in mathematics and about "disciplinary problems"), the fact was that nearly 80% of the first graduating classes from the Scholae Europaeae had either finished their university programs or (in Germany) were moving ahead without difficulty — though the Europe-wide drop-out rate in the first two years of university is well over 50%. The achievement was particularly remarkable as the Scholae Europaeae for compassionate reasons cut a little deeper into the intelligence distribution than any of the national secondary systems in the six Common Market countries. The inspectorates have therefore eased off somewhat in their control of the curriculum and the examinations.

Moreover, like all bureaucracies, the inspectorates are sometimes forgetful. Brussels in 1966–67 was teaching a mathematics program all its own in four of the seven years of secondary school. "There was no mathematics inspector for two years," explained Marcel Desmadryl, assistant headmaster of the Brussels school, "so we took the initiative." A text for the fifth year, prepared in Brussels but approved by the teaching staffs at Luxembourg and Varese (which will presently adopt the program), has been submitted to higher authority and will probably go into the classroom, one book translated into four languages. In history, which is not examined, the teachers of the program for the final year are meeting to develop their own course and write their own book.

The experiment which has involved the greatest number of teachers is an attempt to develop a European literature course to be taught as part of the native language and the first foreign language. A working group of one each from the five larger countries — including a French expert on Spanish literature, a Belgian whose graduate work had been done in Scandinavian literature and a Dutchman with degrees from British universities — put together a number of units on medieval literature to be taught to 15–16-year-olds, in the fifth year. The theme was courtly love — "definitely European in every literature, and for the children definitely attractive," according to one of the committee. Each teacher contributed two suggested texts designed to show both the binding element in the continental literature and specific national features. In telling about the experiment, Bein Poppinga, a Dutch teacher of English in Brussels, said, "The whole theory of the course led us to *la nature britannique*, and in turn to Celtic literature; we found an excellent Welsh text in which a 'lady' was described. The German literature was difficult: in most of the texts the ladies are there just to pour the beer for the warriors, but the Welsh can be translated into chivalrous love. And we have a Dutch fragment in which a knight — a farmer's boy — does not recognize the code. It was written by a townsman: typical of certain facets of Holland. We gave the students the original texts, with translations, that we made or found, into French and German, and we wrote an introduction in the mother tongue to each selection.

"The Middle Ages, of course," Poppinga continued, "were relatively easy. In 1966 we started on the Renaissance and the seventeenth century, and agreed only on three lessons: one on Italian humanism, one on Erasmus and one on Baroque lyrical poetry, a most difficult job of translation. In 1967 we did French classicism and its influence, the early English novel, the Enlightenment."

The shift away from centralized control has been reflected by an easing of the examination structure. The European Baccalaureate is now given in three parts — before Christmas, before Easter and at the end of the year — and for the first two parts the questions are written by the teachers at the schools. In 1967, in most subjects, even the final examination was put together by the inspectorate entirely from questions submitted by the teachers. This mode of operation is foreign to the Latins in the Community but natural to the Germans and Dutch, and it may reflect a slight educational shift away from the French domination visible in the organization and even the architecture of the schools.

First priority for admission to the schools goes to citizens of the six Common Market countries regardless of whether they work for one of the supranational institutions. The schools may admit local children up to but not beyond the number of the largest foreign contingent. (The Belgian government has limited the locals at the Brussels school to children of employees of the supranational organizations; the French have no Schola Europaea on their territory.) Fees range from $10 a year in the kindergarten to $65 a year in the secondary cycles; but the fee includes books, which most Europeans would have to supply for their children in their home countries. Below a certain income level the fees can be waived: the children of Italian laborers, for example, attend without charge. The very difficult problem of what to do for the child who is not university material has been partially solved at the Schola Europaea in Luxembourg by the provision of a "post-primary" program which does not lead to the European Baccalaureate. "That is why I am so highly decorated by the Italian government," said Voss, the German director of the Luxembourg school. Transiency is, of course, a universal handicap to international schools, and the Scholae Europaeae are not exempt: only 30% of the students remain as long as three years.

FROM THE CLASSROOM

At the Schola Europaea in Varese, north of Milan, a class of 15–16-year-olds is studying geography. On a blackboard that swings out from the wall are written the words Rough Riders, Wilson and Philippines Guerre; but this lesson is geography. It is taught in French, to children for whom French is a second language, a "vehicular language." The subject is *les eaux sauvages et les torrents*. The method is the slide lecture, known locally as audio-visual, with the room dark and the teacher working the slide projector himself. "*Mauvaises terres — comment dit-on en anglais? — bad lands — dans les Montagnes Roches....*"

Bad lands and the like are made by violent storms in dry climates. There is a slide of Fairy Canyon — "*comment dit-on en allemand? en italien?*" Sources of erosion are the nature of the rock: "*Terre friable est facilement——*" He pauses for a word from the class, and does not get it. "*Erodée.*" Then there is the slope of the land and the volume of water. By now the class has turned into a catechism, and answers are coming from the students — in one word, not in sentences, but the teacher will take what he can get. Eventually, he begins to lose what is, after all, a middle-class group

The Scholae Europaeae

of adolescents; he snaps on the lights and says, "Distribute the stencil" — and everybody takes a test.

*   *   *

In the Schola Europaea of Brussels, an all-Italian group is studying history in French, with the usual Hachette text, profusely illustrated, typographically confusing. The teacher asks, "What was the catastrophe of the middle fourteenth century?" and gets back the quick answer, "*La peste.*" Today's unit is on city-states. The textbook offers only the Hanseatic cities and the Italian cities; the teacher adds Novgorod, Bergen and Riga. What were the shipping routes? "*Les vins de Bordeaux sont transportés dans les——*" A boy supplies *tonneaux*, and the teacher points out that this is the origin of measuring the capacity of shipping in "tons." We move on to the city-states of Florence, Venice and Ghent, and the question of land traffic, the major route over the Great Saint Bernard and its gradual abandonment. Why? A boy replies, "*Les brigands.*"

Everyone has done his work and functions. Next there are the financial customs, the *lettres de change*, then Bruges, and the notebooks fill with line after line of brute hard information to be stored ready for retrieval on a test. But the notebook itself will be inspected, and the notes are taken, not in the students' native language, but in French.

*   *   *

At the Schola Europaea of Luxembourg, a handsome Italian in later middle age, with white hair and a dark mustache, looking a little like Vittorio De Sica, is putting a baker's dozen of 16- to 18-year-olds through the first class after Easter vacation. The group is Dutch, French and German, and this is their fourth foreign language — Latin, German (or French), English, now Italian. The class meets three times a week, and it is in essence filling out the program. Most of the students have had two years of Italian, but a few have had only one year, and two have had three years.

The teacher asks the class to talk about what they did during vacation. They plow ahead, accustomed to speaking in a language not their own, knowing a little Italian but not much. The teacher jollies them along, keeps them talking. One student spent his vacation reading mystery stories. "Mystery stories" is translated literally into Italian, which is not right. The teacher asks how Italians speak of such literature, gets no answer, and supplies one himself: "*Libri gialli*" — literally, yellow books. The class loves it, and begins playing games in Italian with the possible colors of books.

The teacher comes over to the visitor. "You have to understand," he says, "that this is not examined for on the Baccalaureate. So I must keep them amused...."

CHAPTER 5: **A Multinational Multitude**

Though almost nobody in the English-speaking world has ever heard of them — and their existence is surprisingly little known even inside the Common Market countries — the Scholae Europaeae must be the model for future international schools. They are by some margin the best staffed, the best housed and the best financed of all such institutions, and in program and purpose they are the least accidental. They are, however, very expensive operations, which only governments or intergovernmental agencies can sustain, and the difficulties of starting such schools are obviously formidable. In Europe, the International Atomic Energy Agency has been stalemated in its efforts to launch such a school in either Vienna or Trieste; and in the United States no action has been taken on a very thorough "feasibility study" financed by the International Monetary Fund, the World Bank and the Inter-American Development Bank, which recommended the establishment of a school in Washington, D.C., rather like the Scholae Europaeae (with English, Spanish and French linguistic groups).

The three consultants to the financial agencies were Albert van Houtte of the Scholae Europaeae, Joseph Lauwerys of the University of London (Belgian by nationality) and Clarence Beeby of New Zealand, formerly chairman of the Executive Board of UNESCO and after retirement a research associate at Harvard. Their proposal was for seconded teachers, compulsory courses taught in a working second language, and examinations to "satisfy the conditions of the Common Market Schools."[1] The report was backed by a survey of the Washington international community which demonstrated substantial demand for such a school, and the cause was pressed by Mrs. Dorothy Goodman, an American historian and wife of a British official in the World Bank organization. On the failure of the international agencies to act, Mrs. Goodman started an international nursery school in her own home, planning its expansion into the grades year by year, in hopes that the financial institutions would ultimately make it real. Indeed, the report of the committee has never been rejected, and the project for a Washington school is dormant rather than dead, awaiting a kiss from a Prince Charming with about three million dollars.

One private school may attempt the Schola Europaea model: the International School of The Hague, at present a group of four schools (American, British, French and German) unified only by name, by a common board of trustees that rarely meets and has little to do, and by an extraordinarily competent one-day-a-week director, a lively, wry Dutchman named Jan Van Der Valk.

Founded in 1953 as a single school with national sections,

---

[1] *Proposals to Establish an International School in Washington: Feasibility Study*, 1965, Vol. II, p. 68.

A Multinational Multitude

the International School of The Hague gradually split into four separate institutions, each in its own building. Van Der Valk, who had been head of a Dutch overseas school in Switzerland, was then head of a Quaker international school in financial difficulties ("it couldn't break even on one hundred children or hold more than one hundred"). The Quaker school asked the municipality of The Hague to take over, and the city fathers after examining the situation told the Quakers that they didn't want the school but they did want Van Der Valk for their floundering secular International School. Van Der Valk ran it until 1961, when he was offered the director's job at the city's best high school — the science and modern-language (no classics) comprehensive school. His successor was unable to ride the four horses, and in 1963 Van Der Valk was asked to return. ("Nobody else was crazy enough to take a hard job at a very low salary.") He had recommended, at his departure, that the school break juridically into separate institutions, as it had practically, but all four communities refused. Van Der Valk undertook to resume the leadership of the International School only on a basis where each section would provide its own principal and he would try to coordinate efforts in his spare time.

As of the mid-1960s, the American branch had about 600 students, the British about 250, and the French and German about 200 each. Teachers for the American and British schools were privately recruited; for the French and German schools, they were supplied (and paid) by the embassies. The British government did, however, inspect the British school, and arrangements had been made for teachers there to retain their seniority rights and pensions in their home jobs. At the French and German schools, about half the students were permanent; the length of stay was two to three years at the American and British schools.

Reunification of these four schools seemed improbable but not impossible. Van Der Valk's plan for the future called for a new building to house all four, to be built at a cost of about two million dollars. The municipality of The Hague had agreed to donate the land, and the first $700,000 of construction money had been pledged by the U. S. State Department. The building would consist of four connected wings of three stories each, organized vertically by nationality and horizontally by age group, with a handful of shared laboratory, library and recreational facilities. The different national managements would then have the option of keeping their students separate or mixing them in patterns similar to those of the Scholae Europaeae. Van Der Valk believes that propinquity would promote cooperation — especially if somebody could supply an international university entrance examination toward which all students could work in the secondary years.

2

Another kind of international school is the institution operated primarily for local residents but accommodating through various special devices the children of a foreign community. By definition, these schools prepare students for the local university-entrance examinations. The courtesies extended on the examination may range from zero (as at the former NATO lycées, where everyone was expected to compete on the French *baccalauréat*, with an added exam in their own literature and history for the foreigners), through substantial (at the Nicolaus Cusanus Gymnasium in Bad Godesberg, near Bonn, where candidates for the *Abitur* are allowed to use their own language for most of a largely oral exam) to major (in Sweden, where the entire exam is translated into English for the benefit of the foreign candidate and special

A Multinational Multitude

"international" literature and history courses are substituted for the national program).

Most such schools find themselves unable to carry their foreign students through secondary education. Thus the international section at the experimental lycée in Sèvres has been confined to the first four-year cycle of the French secondary system. The section was started in 1960, with some help from UNESCO, which demanded bilingual classes and priority in admission for the children of UNESCO employees. Only a hundred children attend altogether, 20 of them from UNESCO. In 1965 there were 22 nationalities represented in the school. The largest single contingent was American (30), followed by a group regarded as French because one parent was French (the other was foreign and employed by an international or foreign organization). "The Americans dominate," said Mme Quignard, the *directrice* of the international section, "because the business firms send people here for a long time." After the UNESCO obligation is met, the international section of Sèvres looks first for students whose parents can pledge their attendance for the full four years. About 40% of the students do stay the course, and the rest turn over, some annually because their parents are visiting professors. This is a state school; there is no tuition charge.

At the end of their bilingual four years, American students take the College Board aptitude test and perhaps a few achievement tests (though at 15 or 16 they are too young for college); the British take O-level G.C.E. (a year or so early) in most subjects, and A-level G.C.E. French. The school says the results are good, but does not report specifics. Students in the international section are segregated in a wooden shack at the foot of the hill on which stands the modern lycée, but they mix with the lycée students for music and art and library and lunch. The academic program is roughly that of the parent lycée, with its emphasis on concrete objects and progressive methods — concrete and progressive, that is, by French standards.

Language instruction in both English and French (and more than a quarter of the school usually needs intensive work in both, because a third language is spoken at home) is given at splendidly equipped language laboratories in the main building, with heavy use of tapes, slides and closed-circuit television. No native English-speaking faculty is employed (only French nationals may be on the payroll of the Ministry of Education), but several of the teachers are effectively bilingual. Mathematics and experimental science courses are taught in both French and English; other courses, in French alone. A single teacher handles students for both French and history, on the grounds that he knows their vocabulary problems.

Most people associated with the international section would like to see it expand into the second cycle, but the Ministry of Education feels that children from this background should not be asked to attempt the standard *baccalauréat*, which is all a French school can offer. In 1967, the Ministry agreed in principle to establish the section on a full seven-year basis if an international university entrance examination could be created and pushed through to general acceptance.

3

Except for the former NATO lycées, which may or may not have a future, the only official state school organized specifically to carry foreigners through the examination of the host country is the Nicolaus Cusanus Gymnasium in Bad Godesberg. Housed in an unusually handsome glass-and-concrete building with a spectacular view of the Seven Mountains across the Rhine, the school was opened in 1951 as a service

A Multinational Multitude 117

to the growing embassy community and the national civil service. It has about 900 students, of whom about 180 are foreigners, 40 to 50 of them permanent and the rest mostly on two-year tours of duty. The foreign contingent is not permitted to make up more than a quarter of the school. In 1965, 34 nationalities were represented.

Students who enter between the ages of 10 and 14 are expected to follow a completely German program once they leave reception classes, where they remain for six months to two years; students in this age bracket who have not learned enough German to transfer to normal classes after two years are, in the words of Dr. H. Breier, *Oberstudiendirektor* of the school, "dismissed." About 15% to 25% fall in this category. In the reception classes the students work on "German for foreigners, English for foreigners and math for foreigners."

There are no reception classes for students entering over the age of 14, but they may take "German for foreigners" while their classmates are at music, art and physical education. These students are permitted to take part of the *Abitur* in their own language, a favor which the school regards seriously — a few years ago a professor of Japanese was found to help examine a Japanese girl. German is then examined as a first foreign language. As a special courtesy, Latin is not required of the foreign candidates, "because in our experience," Dr. Breier said, "no foreign candidate has ever passed *Abitur* Latin, except one American — he is famous." The 180 foreigners produce only about half a dozen *Abitur* candidates a year.

FROM
THE CLASSROOM

At the NATO lycée at Saint-Germain-en-Laye, a young man out of a French movie about secondary school life — long-haired, lean, interestingly ugly, with big horn-rimmed glasses — is racing a *classe de Philo* (in the last year, 18 years old, and taking humanities rather than science) through a syllabus in European geography. He lectures in French, very systematically, *premièrement, deuxièmement*, etc.

"In Belgium and Holland there were no peasants: the farms are too near the cities. In Holland more than forty per cent live in cities of more than thirty thousand; in Belgium, more than fifty per cent." He writes on the board, *Randstaad Holland*. "Ensemble of Rotterdam, Amsterdam, The Hague — the only example in Europe of three large cities less than thirty kilometers apart. Amsterdam has nine hundred thousand population, *le Venise du Nord*, great historic city, *maisons particuliers*, great center of colonial industries, also the great financial center. *Voilà pour Amsterdam*." Rotterdam has a population of 700,000. It's a port, great commercial center, great modern city. Destroyed 1940 by bombs, now great experiment in building a modern city. Remarkably organized. Like Düsseldorf a commercial capital. The Hague is another thing: 500,000 population, administrative center, *ville de résidence, la cour*. . . . "*Voilà le Randstaad Holland.*"

We move to Belgium. Pens fly over blue notebooks. Antwerp is the Flemish center, Liège the French center; population figures; "Brussels plays the role of Paris. The 1958 World's Fair showed the prosperity of liberal capitalism.

"Now we have finished the lesson on geography. Get your history books. The Weimar Republic, 1919–1933. What was the essence of the Weimar? An incomplete defeat; an incomplete revolution." The name Ebert appears on the board. "The military — you must understand the mentality of the Germans — the military say, 'You kept us from winning the war.' Their armies were still in France. They did not see the defeat. There was an attempt at a Communist Revolution in 1918." On the board appear the further names Spartacus, Liebknecht, Rosa Luxemburg, Eisner. The piece of chalk returns to the name Liebknecht: "You remember him from last year — the father founded the Social Democratic Party. The Army was at the service of the Ministry of the Interior." On the board appears the name Noske; and again we have the

A Multinational Multitude

phrase: "the incomplete defeat, the incomplete revolution." Clearly, this slogan *must* be written in the notes.

Next, the Weimar Constitution: the liberal spirit of Goethe; "a beautiful constitution"; its great merit for the Germans being that it maintained the unity of Germany. *Deuxièmement*, the separation of powers: *"Le Reichstag fait le rat — le Reichsrat."* The President of the Republic elected for seven years, designates a Prime Minister called the Chancellor. Article 48 of the Constitution provides . . . *"Voilà la Constitution Weimar en gros."*

All the 18-year-olds are glancing out the window at the beautiful fall day, but their hands are working, making notes.

*   *   *

"There was this film that was imagined by Alec Guinness," says the teacher of English at the international section of the Lycée de Sèvres, "about the mouth of the horse. . . ."

4

Though they were founded and are still largely run by Europeans (only a few of whom have been nationalized), the international schools of black Africa should also be slotted in the category of national schools with foreign sections. A major purpose in founding these schools was the expansion of educational resources for middle-class nationals of the host country. They are monolingual in the language used by the state schools of the locality, a good chunk of their pupil population is local, and they prepare students for the same examinations as the local schools. (The Ghana International School in Accra sits the O-level London University G.C.E. rather than the examination for the West African School Certificate, but so do most Ghanaian secondary schools.) As Africa grows increasingly inhospitable to white residents, it seems inevitable that the international schools will come under increasing domination by the local authorities.

At Ibadan in Nigeria the international school is officially the property of the University of Ibadan and unofficially the particular pet of Andrew Taylor, a New Zealander, professor of education, pukka sahib in immaculate whites, whose son was at Gordonstoun when he decided there ought to be a school on the university grounds. Ibadan's headmaster in 1965, D. S. Snell, had been assistant headmaster at Gordonstoun; about one-third of the staff of 26 (for 280 students) were British, one-third American and one-third Nigerian. The school buildings were put up with about $225,000 of U. S. A.I.D. money, $140,000 of Ford Foundation money, and $28,000 from the Western Region of Nigeria, on land owned by the university.

The first class entered in 1963, and alumni are still scarce. The school takes children at age 11-plus and provides six years for Americans or seven for the English and Nigerians, to the A-level West African School Certificate. Roughly 120 of the students in 1965 were boarders, nearly all from families living in Lagos, where no secondary education is offered as yet to the children of foreigners. Fees for boarders were about $1,250 a year, all included. A large proportion of the Nigerian student group at the school was Ibo in origin. If as a result of the recent civil war the University of Ibadan and its school were to become a Yoruba fief in the African tribal pattern, it seems unlikely that either could survive as a significant institution. One thing the school had in 1965 was ambition — "this sort of thing must be high quality for *anywhere*," said Taylor "or it isn't worth doing, don't you know?"

Uncertainty as to its current status also makes it difficult to write about the Ghana International School in Accra, which in 1965 boasted that two of Nkrumah's children were among the students. (Not actually at the school, of course — not in

A Multinational Multitude

a socialist democracy — but teachers from the school were charged with the duty of visiting the palace and educating the Redeemer's offspring.) Mrs. Eleanor Boateng, an English elementary teacher married to a minister in the Nkrumah government, was the assistant headmistress. Unlike most international schools, the Accra school had a fairly large contingent of Eastern Europeans; they outnumbered the Anglo-American group, which comprised less than a fifth of the 600 or so students. But the secondary school, which carried students only to O-level on the G.C.E., was two-thirds American, Canadian and Indian.

The Accra school acquired its first science laboratory only in the latter half of 1964, and in areas like mathematics and grammar its practice was about forty years behind current methodology in England. Social studies work, however, was infused with a naïve Marxism that made a refreshing contrast to the naïve liberalism typical of other international schools. Moreover, the presence of non-English-speaking Poles and Czechs and Hungarians made it necessary for the school to establish a reception class to teach English to newcomers. "The middle-European children," said Mrs. Boateng admiringly, "are so quick and hard-working that they often leave for the regular classes at the end of one term." The school ran mornings only, "because it gets hot here in the afternoon," and classes were held 43 weeks a year, in three terms divided by three three-week vacations. "Parents' leave comes at different times, and this way nobody misses a whole term."

FROM
THE CLASSROOM

At the Ghana International School, a rather formidable English lady is moving vigorously through the problems of English punctuation, marching along the blackboard as she writes sample sentences.

"As I've told you, anything you can put between two commas is usually something you can leave out. Adjectival clauses that are necessary you cannot use commas for." Most of the children in this class of 12-year-olds are not natively English-speaking; they are rooted to their chairs, looking straight ahead with glazed expressions. "You should be able to do that in your sleep — what is the role of the coordinating conjunction?" No answer. She writes on the board, quoting herself as she writes: " 'They always said that, and they said no more.' That's an optional comma — you can put it in and you can leave it out."

Finally the children are asked to read from their textbook, which is very, very English. "Do you all know what a temperance hotel is? Does anybody know what a non-conformist is? Well, that's what I meant when I told you this book is insular. It doesn't bear much relation to your experience." The people in the story are on a hike, and one of the ladies is wearing "hosiery, elastic webs and boots." The teacher pauses reminiscently: "I remember," she says, "that's what we wore in the Army...."

5

In the Scandinavian countries, where private schools are subsidized, the governments as a matter of course offer the same subsidy for foreign and native enrollments in secular and Lutheran but not Catholic schools. There is an old-established French school in Stockholm, Cour Saint Louis, a Catholic foundation, with students of 31 nationalities, all girls, and with a social cachet which may be indicated by the fact that the King sent his daughter (but with no subsidy at all from the Swedish government — "Our Swedish girls," said Fröken Elisabeth Carrier, its *directrice*, a Catholic nun in mufti, "even have to pay for their own *lunch*."). All other Scandinavian secondary schools for the international community are a creation of the mid-1960s.

The only one within bus distance of Stockholm is a graft on

A Multinational Multitude

the established Stiftelsen Viggbyholmskolan, an upper-class boarding school fifteen or so miles from town. Students are accepted into the international section at age 16 for the last three years of secondary education, with courses offered in English; as of 1966 there were 50 students enrolled. English and American textbooks are used for all subjects except French, where the staff found nothing it considered satisfactory and made its own translation of the standard Swedish textbook for teaching French. In 1966-67, a once-a-week course in philosophy (!) was offered to the English section of the school in Swedish, and one class on the Swedish side studied biology in English. The school must, of course, recruit its own teachers; and the problem of finding competent and experienced English-speaking staff for so small a group has not been solved. The outstanding teacher in 1965 was an Indian national who had become a British barrister and somehow found himself in Stockholm. In 1967-68, the departure of its headmaster, following arguments over the future of the international section, left the role of the English-speaking group in doubt.

In Copenhagen the municipality has turned over to a parents' group based on the American Embassy some rooms in a new John F. Kennedy Elementary School, to house what is called the "Copenhagen International School." Ulf Østergaard, director of the nearby Soborg Gymnasium and former head of the United Nations School in New York, is helping with the planning and would like to see a full secondary section emerge in time. The established school for foreigners in Copenhagen, however, is still the Bernadotteskolen, private and "progressive" as nothing in the homeland of progressivism still is. There are about 500 students in the Bernadotteskolen, and 60 of them are in the English-speaking section. The school runs only through ninth grade, after which visiting Americans are encouraged to attempt correspondence courses offered by the University of Nebraska.

The Bernadotteskolen international community is highly transient — about 18 months is the average stay — and no serious effort has been made to build an academic program. Students are told to obtain the books they would be using if they had stayed home, and somebody on the staff will help them through the material. The administrator of the English section is Ted Duval, a young Floridian who came to the University of Copenhagen to do graduate work in Icelandic sagas and made some friends who had children in the school.

Both teachers and children switch activities a good deal during the day, according to what interests them at the moment, and there is heavy emphasis on "workshops." The air is affrighted, for example, with the sounds of the jazz workshop, which goes all morning — one girl playing trumpet, another bent over a piano, boys in assorted lounging attitudes playing clarinet, saxophone and drums, and the teacher plucking a bull fiddle while he leans against the wall, cigarette drooping from his mouth. In 1965 the school was debating whether or not to pioneer a five-day week in Denmark, where all schools run Monday through Saturday. "The majority of the parents want the five-day week," Duval said, "but seventy per cent of the children are opposed. My second-graders say they want to come Sundays, too."

Because the Danish government gives an 80% subvention, fees are only about $15 a month, and there is a waiting list for places. There is no prospect of a secondary section at the school, however, and no interest whatever in things like examinations; until 1963 the school did not even prepare its Danish students for the standard *Realexamen* for entrance into *Gymnasium*, because the staff disapproved of such formalities. Now, "because the exam has been liberalized," courses leading to *Gymnasium* are offered, even including physics, and three-quarters of the Danish children are in examination programs in grades 8 and 9. Foreigners drift in and out. Though the system is probably not capable of extension, there is no reason to believe that any bright child's education is harmed by the casual approach of the Bernadotteskolen; but, of course, a number of parents were worried.

6

Perhaps the outstanding example of a school basically for local children but especially hospitable to foreigners is the Ecole Active Bilingue in Paris, which in fact considers itself an "international school" and has joined the International Schools Association. Its guiding genii are Mme Rachel Cohen, a professional educator with a license in Philosophy and experience in kindergartens, and Mme Janine Manuel, a Resistance heroine, mother, psychologist and theoretician of the teaching of languages, whose husband, an equally bilingual businessman, has supported her experiments. The school is located in the heart of Paris in a converted private residence which was given to Mme Manuel for a school in recognition of her wartime service to France. The building, a national monument, cannot be greatly altered, but in the courtyard Mme Manuel has built a glass-and-wood tower which houses the project to develop her tape-recorder-*cum*-filmstrip methods for teaching a second language to very young children. A second school building, for the early secondary years, is away from the center of the city, among the luxury housing.

Classwork is in French at the Ecole Active Bilingue, and new students go to reception classes until their French is up to the school's standards. Sixty per cent of the 700 students are French, about thirty per cent are American, and the others are scattered among almost 30 nationalities. Turnover is relatively light: the average stay of non-French-speaking students is four years. "After two years," Mme Cohen says, "you can treat the Americans pedagogically as French."

The experimental language program to date is for the teaching of English (and, more recently and tentatively, Spanish) to French children. Still, a good part of every day is devoted to lessons in English language and culture; and the atmosphere, with a minimum of rote repetition and a maximum of activities (as the name of the school implies), is considerably less of a strain for foreigners than the antique proceedings of the usual French *école primaire*. The curriculum is described as "topic-centered." An oddity of Mme Manuel's method is that the teacher is not supposed to be bilingual herself: the program controls absolutely the lessons and the progression of ideas and materials.

The atmosphere of the school is largely dictated by the background of its strong proprietress. Mme Manuel is one-quarter American, granddaughter of an American painter who settled near Grenoble. She was bilingual virtually from birth, and she sees the internationalism of the education at her school in almost exclusively linguistic terms. In her opinion "international understanding is mostly a matter of learning a number of languages when young." She is not necessarily wrong. Under pressure from parents and from her own unending personal curiosity, Mme Manuel is extending her school into the secondary level. She has been personally active in the work for an international examination, and if this quest finds its grail the Ecole Active Bilingue will be among the schools preparing students to take the test.

7

For the rest there are oddities, religious schools, proprietary schools, indescribable schools rather like a scene from a Graham Greene entertainment. Professor Joseph Lauwerys of the University of London has estimated that Switzerland alone

A Multinational Multitude

has 300 proprietary "international schools," which he describes as "private profit-making institutions often relying on snob appeal." Few of these are selective on entrance. "We have kids from Hong Kong and Pakistan, and Saudi Arabia," said David Nelson of Oregon while academic head of the English side at the Collège du Léman. "They just can't make it and eventually fold up. We have Kirsten X, who finds English immensely difficult and is taking O-level English; her mother says she wishes they had technical schools in Denmark. But some public school philosophy has rubbed off on these places; and, of course, business is business."

Yet some of these establishments are impressively good schools. Le Rosey, for example, a boys' school situated for two of its three terms on large but not especially lavish grounds off the road between Geneva and Lausanne — and for the third term in the skiing country around Gstaad — has been amusingly written up in magazines as a haven for the children of celebrities, aristocracy and even royalty; but the foundation of its success is a first-rate, no-nonsense academic program which pretty much guarantees all students success on their own national examinations. There are about 180 boys in the school, ranging in age from 9 to 18. Nobody is taken without a guarantee that the boy will attend for at least two years, and nobody who declares an intention to take a university entrance examination will be admitted during the last three years. About 30 new students are selected each year from about 800 applicants — a good number, considering that the fees run roughly $3,000 a year.

For the first three years of the program at Le Rosey all instruction is in French; thereafter the school splits into English-speaking and French-speaking sections. Everybody takes history of art and philosophy in French, and a number of boys on the English side take the full French language program on the French side. The school is completely mixed for all extracurricular, recreational and domestic activities. Native language is offered to everyone. In 1965, German, Latin, Italian and Spanish were offered generally as part of the regular program; Russian, Arabic, Flemish, modern Greek, Persian and Swedish were taught in tutoring sessions (free of charge) after school. "We would teach ancient Greek," said Jean Johannot, the director of the school, "but nobody has asked for it in thirteen or fourteen years."

The teaching staff is nearly as international as the pupil population: in 1965, Swiss, French, German, Italian, Swedish, Canadian, American and British nationalities were represented in the full-time staff of 33; Persian, Egyptian and (White) Russian in the part-time staff.

The school week consists of 42 45-minute class periods, some of them set aside for study. On the French side at the end of the first cycle of secondary education (age 16), 38 of the 42 periods are used for instruction. Any energy remaining is sopped up by organized athletics.

What is perhaps most remarkable about Le Rosey is the quality of its mathematics instruction, which is supervised (and in part performed) by Johannot himself. A blunt, rather rough Swiss who will not hesitate to tell a royal Duke that his boy can't make it, Johannot had his own secondary schooling at the International School of Geneva, went on to secure licenses in mathematics and psychology at the University of Geneva and a doctorate under the supervision of Jean Piaget. His dissertation was on mathematical reasoning in the adolescent; and he is a brilliant carrot-and-stick teacher of math. The median score on the College Board verbal Scholastic Aptitude Test at Le Rosey in 1965 was about 540, which was highly creditable for a group containing a number of students whose native language was not English. The median score on the mathematical part of the test was over 650, and perfect performance was commonplace.

Le Rosey will prepare for any examination the student must take, with perhaps one exception: the Italian *maturitá*. A few years ago several staff members waited around through a hot early July to play their role with visiting Italian inspectors in the oral part of the *maturitá*. Despite a firm date, the Italians didn't show up; and for the time being Le Rosey's attitude toward the *maturitá* is, to hell with it.

At almost the opposite pole is (or maybe was) the International School of Milan, a sort of non-profit proprietary day school owned by Francesco Formiga, a former functionary of the city of Milan who speaks only Italian but grew wealthy on a chain of commercial schools which train Italian girls to be English-language secretaries for British and American industry in north Italy. Pleased with their secretaries, these employers came to Formiga with the complaint that there was no school in all northern Italy for their children and the suggestion that he remedy the defect. The school opened in 1959 with 35 pupils and rapidly expanded to more than 300. Fortunately, the archdiocese had put up a new school building not far from the center of town without a prior survey of the demand for confessional education in the neighborhood, and there was thus a surplus school plant for rent. With the 1964-65 school year, the rather small secondary section (about 75 students in grades 9-13) moved over to quarters in the business district formerly occupied by the secretarial schools.

Five full-time teachers carried most of the load in the secondary division — a science teacher trained at the University of London, a social studies and American English teacher trained at Harvard, an English English teacher trained at Glasgow, an Egyptian mathematics teacher from the French university in Beirut and an Egyptian French teacher from the

University of Cairo. Two Italians filled in part-time to teach Italian (required of all students) and Latin. The language of instruction was English, and the curriculum was largely that of the London University G.C.E., though there were occasional devoirs to the College Boards.

Though administrative procedure at the International School of Milan was remarkably slipshod — between 1959 and 1966 there were five different principals — the ability of the teachers made up in large part for the transiency of both the management and the students. As a money-losing operation, however, the school was in constant danger of extinction by its parent organization, the chain of secretarial schools whose profits it diminished; and on the elementary level its functions were being put in question by a new American Community School started by a group of parents and teachers from the International School.

8

A few international schools, none complete through the secondary years, have been set up by private enterprises financed and staffed from several countries and situated in remote areas. Perhaps the most remarkable of these is the school at Yekepa, at the Nimba iron mines in the backwoods of Liberia (which is saying a great deal). Lamco, the sponsoring company, is owned jointly by the Liberian government, Sweden's giant Grangesberg Corporation and America's Bethlehem Steel, and is financed in part from West Germany. Wishing to hire engineers, administrators, skilled machinists and operatives from many countries, the Swedish administration of the project decided in 1962 to run an English-language school for all children 14 and under, staffed about one-third by Swedish teachers skilled in English. Books are mostly English,

A Multinational Multitude

occasionally American. "The broader the company can make the basis for the recruiting program," said Harry Holmberg, a Swedish county supervisor who became principal of the Yekepa school when the shift to English was made, "the better for the company."

This arrangement was satisfactory to the Swedes, who are the dominant national group (158 of 282 children in 1965) for the elementary grades, but they demanded preparation in Swedish for the *Realexamen* (which granted entry to *Gymnasium*) for students above the age of 12. With pressure from the management and changes in the Swedish school system (which now keeps all children together in the same school to age 16), the school has recently been able to extend its English-language program into the secondary grades. The system of the NATO lycées — six hours a week in native language for everybody — has guaranteed a sufficient continuity with home conditions for students whose parents are on a one- or two-year contract. As virtually nobody lives in Yekepa except employees of Lamco, the native Liberian population consists entirely of the children of white-collar and highly skilled workers at the mine.

Because the costs of running the school are so small compared with the tens of millions of dollars invested in the mine and its railroad, the school building and equipment are excellent, complete to an air-conditioned storage room to protect books and supplies from the climate. But it is hard to get staff to Yekepa, even at high salaries; and both staff and students suffer from isolation and transiency. The school is a member of the International Schools Association, and Lamco would rather like to add a full secondary division, to hold certain key employees. But for now there is enough trouble running a program which will equip students (some of them from homes of only rudimentary education) to return at age 14 to their own national secondary systems.

CHAPTER 6: **The French Foreign Lycées**

Some 35,000 teachers on the payroll of the French government are working in some 600 schools outside the French Empire. Most of them are maintaining the French presence in former French colonies, in Africa and Indo-China and Quebec, but several thousand are working in schools — French-owned and foreign-owned, official and private and even proprietary, secular and religious — in countries where the official language is not French. The budget for this effort — not much short of $200 million a year, most of it in teacher salaries — is greater than all the rest of the expenses of the Ministry of Foreign Affairs put together.

Nothing in education is more spectacular or more admirable than the brilliance and flexibility of the French *lycées d'outre-mer*. In at least thirty significant cities around the world, the best school in town is the French lycée; and the political, social and intellectual leaders of the place are convinced that the highest of the world's cultures is that of France. With only two exceptions — in Istanbul and Teheran — the French lycée overseas offers a program leading to the same *baccalauréat* that will be taken in metropolitan France. (For the South American lycées the University of Toulouse prepares a separate examination to be administered in November rather than in June; equivalence is guaranteed.) But where national requirements must be met by local students, the lycée will also prepare its charges for the national examination. This must be done not only in far-away places like Montevideo and São Paulo, but also in neighboring cities like London and Madrid.

The suppleness and subtlety with which the Ministry of Foreign Affairs handles its educational funds can be appreciated only when the different schools in the budget are considered in some detail. Apparently, only two requirements are absolute: the language of instruction must be French, and the school must be willing to accept inspection from metropolitan France at intervals of three to five years.

"We try to help in every possible way, according to the local laws," said G. Tallon, second-in-command at the Education Office in the Ministry. "In the nineteenth century the lycée could simply be transported, with the same courses and the same exams as in France. This is not possible — it is not *desirable* — today. Our new treaties recognize that secondary programs are different from country to country. So we have to negotiate not only with the foreign countries but also with our own Ministry of Education."

Normally, relations between the two ministries are excellent. The Ministry of Education advertises all vacancies in the overseas lycées, processes and screens the applicants, enabling this vast foreign educational effort to be run by a staff of only 70 (including secretaries) in Paris. People who apply for any one post are held to have applied for all, and the Min-

The French Foreign Lycées

istry of Foreign Affairs takes them in hand. "The new ones," said Tallon, "always want Italy or Spain. We tell them, 'No. But we have a nice place for you in Malawi or Honduras.'" Those who are taken into the foreign lycées are detached from the national system, but retain all seniority and pension rights and benefits. The maximum tour in any one place is six years: "If you keep him too long in Japan and Mexico he will become Japanese and Mexican." Though many teachers in the overseas lycées remain out of France for most of their working lives, moving to another overseas school when one tour ends, the government does not consider teaching abroad to be a separate career. Many teachers (and *proviseurs*) transfer in and out of France regularly. Tallon said, "We want to keep it *perméable*."

Recruitment is aided by the national military service law, which excuses those who sign up to teach three years in an overseas school. Of the 35,000 teachers abroad in 1967, nearly 9,000 were fulfilling military obligations (at military salary scales); and perhaps as many more first came into the overseas system through this gate. Still, every year there are many more applicants than openings. The teachers in the foreign lycées regard themselves as an elite corps, chosen to serve national purposes while they see the world. They are right, too. What illuminates the French overseas educational effort is the *esprit de corps* of the immensely able and justly proud teachers who carry abroad the culture of their homeland without the slightest doubt that those to whom they carry it want it.

2

The ideal overseas lycée, from the French point of view, is the Lycée Chateaubriand in Rome, which was started in 1904 by the resident French community and adopted by the French government in 1918. Until World War II it served the local

French and foreigners who had taken their previous studies in a French-speaking atmosphere; at no time were there more than 150 students. After the war, the first Gaullist government negotiated a cultural treaty with Italy, by which both countries recognized the validity for their own nationals of the Italian *liceo* in Paris and the French lycée in Rome; and Italians began to apply to the Chateaubriand.

As of 1967, the school had 1,200 students in attractive buildings at opposite ends of the city. About 750 of the students were Italians, who in addition to the *baccalauréat* program took three hours a week of Italian language, literature, culture, history and geography, taught by teachers sent (and paid) by the Italian Ministry of Public Instruction. Some 250 students were French nationals, and the 200 others were distributed among 39 other nationalities, Americans leading with about 35. The Food and Agriculture Organization, which has its headquarters in Rome, is a major source of pupils. Some notion of the local reputation of the school may be gathered from the fact that at one point in this decade, despite the presence of several American and several British schools in the city, the children of both the American and the British ambassadors were enrolled in the Lycée Chateaubriand.

The French government maintains the buildings and sends 30-odd of the 50-odd teachers, plus the entire administrative staff; the remaining expenses are covered by an annual fee of about $200 a child. There are no scholarships. When asked the family background of the Italian students, the *proviseur* said, "Theatre and movies, journalists, doctors, lawyers — professional people." Local children are accepted only at ages 3 and 4 unless they have been to French lycées abroad. French children from state schools are automatically placed in the grades where they would be if they were home; French children from private or religious schools and all other foreigners must take a test. "It is hard for the foreign students," said

The French Foreign Lycées

the *proviseur*, "but if they work *obstinately* they can succeed."

The program offered is precisely that of the metropolitan French lycée, except that English (*not* Italian) is required of Italian students as a first foreign language. In the last year, more than two-thirds of the school is in the humanities option; neither the experimental sciences option (mostly useful for admission to medical faculties) nor the new economics-politics option was offered in 1967. "Virtually all" candidates pass the *baccalauréat*. "Because we are not too big," said the *proviseur*, "we can choose students. If they have difficulty we advise the parents to withdraw them. Those who finish have the ability and the will."

The Chateaubriand conforms in one way to the custom of the country. Italian public schools operate mornings only, and send children home for the day around one o'clock. The French schedule cannot be met on this timetable, and the compromise is to give all academic classes in the morning, reserving physical education, art and music for the afternoon, when attendance is expected but is not compulsory. Not the least of the attractions of a post in this school for the French overseas teacher — the Lycée Chateaubriand is by some margin the first choice of all who apply to the Ministry of Foreign Affairs — is the fact of free afternoons in Rome. By contrast, incidentally, the lycée in Vienna (another place where local schools operate mornings only) runs from 8:30 to 4:00, with lunch at school; its *proviseur* considers the all-day schedule a major reason why parents apply: "They want a baby-sitter."

FROM
THE CLASSROOM

At the Lycée Chateaubriand in Rome, a class of 35 non-Italians, ages 12 and 13, are studying Italian with a young lady who tells the visitor she is French and is surely truthful, but could not be more Italian in intonation, manner or attitude. She speaks nothing but

Italian to the class, which is mostly French but includes five Americans, a Portuguese, Israelis, Czechs, Vietnamese and a Norwegian. Some of them were born in Rome and have a lot of Italian; others are taking the second year of an entirely foreign language.

The lesson opens with a boy at the blackboard, translating into Italian, sentence by sentence, a business letter which a girl reads aloud to him in French. Each sentence is thrown open for discussion and correction, which comes from the class with only minimal intervention by the teacher, who cannot, however, avoid an occasional expression of dismay — as when the boy is revealed not to know the subjunctive forms of *volere*.

Literature comes next, a poem by Gozzano about antiquarianism. A few explanations are necessary — *figura* in Italian means the entire figure, and is not the equivalent of *figure* in French, which means just the face. The poem describes mosaics. Where has the class seen mosaics? A number of Roman churches are mentioned; and the Israeli boy has seen some at home. Everybody speaks Italian, with varying degrees of difficulty. The teacher tells stories from Italian history and Roman gossip to point up phrases in the poem, then moves on to its form — a line of eighteen syllables, not elegant, "*versi barbari*."

On demand by the visitor, the teacher explains herself (in Italian). There were no Italians in her family: she fell in love with the language while at lycée back home, then studied it at the University of Lyons, under a professor who required his students to spend at least twelve months in Italy before he would give them their final examination. She came summers and Easter vacations, living with Italian families; of her entering class at Lyons, she was the only one given the diploma in Italian. When she applied for duty at the Lycée Chateaubriand, the usual rules reserving such places for experienced teachers were glady waived.

3

At the other end of the old Axis, in Berlin, the official French lycée is the Französischer Gymnasium, located in new buildings in the area set aside for the homes of the wives and

The French Foreign Lycées

families of the French part of the army that still in theory occupies the city. Across the street is Berlin's busy French airport; at some future time the school is to be moved to larger quarters in a quieter place.

The Französischer Gymnasium is the successor to an establishment 275 years old, endowed by a King of Prussia for the benefit of the Huguenots fleeing France. After a while the city ran out of Huguenots, but the school continued to function as a French-speaking secondary school for German students within the context of the Berlin public school system. The building was located in what became the Soviet Zone, and when the West Berlin city government decided to revive the Französischer Gymnasium everything had to be started again from scratch. In 1952, the French occupying forces set up their own lycée and, in the words of Horst Schneider, the German administrator of the school, "Somebody had the bright idea of fusion." This was an immensely idealistic venture, still part of the time when Franco-German rapprochement marked the end of war forever, not the preservation of a new power bloc.

In 1965 there were about 700 students in the school. About 420 were Germans and 280 French; no other nationalities were represented. The school took students from the age of 10, in the German pattern of secondary education, and for the first two years the nationality groups were separated. Beyond the age of 12, the entire program was in French, most of it taught, however, by German nationals, who outnumbered the French nationals on the staff by 30 to 12. The two groups of students were mixed for history, Latin, geography, biology, physical education — and French, where the German students were expected to meet *baccalauréat* standards. They were taught separately in German and also (though both groups functioned in French) for mathematics, physics, chemistry and English.

The number of problems this school has solved (or at least has wrestled with) is a catalogue of the difficulties of binational education. To begin with, there is the disparity of ages between French and German students. The French start school at age 5 and the Germans at age 6, and the German pattern in effect gives six years of primary education as against five years for the French. In most classes, the French are a year and a half to two years younger than their German classmates. Schneider said a little wistfully, "We think that perhaps French children develop faster."

In many subjects there are difficulties with text materials. For German students of mathematics, the school can use French texts only through the tenth grade; thereafter, the teachers must write their own. "The French teach solid geometry," said the head of the mathematics department, "and we don't. They use more difficult problems in elementary geometry. They get more quickly to analytic geometry and calculus. In the classics program, the French have only two hours of math a week and we have four. . . ." Many German teachers at the school taught French as a foreign language before coming here, and now they find themselves using their French to teach subjects which are remote from their own academic background. In the case of mathematics, Schneider managed to cut this Gordian knot: he got his hands on an East German refugee mathematics teacher who knew no French, and sent him for two years to the Sorbonne at the expense of the West Berlin government. Music and art, which are "European subjects" at the Scholae Europaeae, are divided subjects here, because the French are unwilling to supply teachers of these subjects to German students or to permit their children to learn these subjects from German teachers.

History has been internationalized essentially by giving French texts to German teachers, who work with both na-

The French Foreign Lycées

tionalities. "Some people complain about bias," Schneider said, "but it is not true — of course, the books are entirely objective. It would be good if there were something more international, but who is to write it? Certainly not us Germans."

Organizationally, too, the two sides of the school are quite different. The French side has its own *proviseur* and *censeur*, who are administrators, pure and simple, but Schneider teaches half a day on five of the six days of the school week. "To tell you the truth," he said, "I don't envy my French colleague who has nothing but red tape."

Some extraordinary compromises have been made here by the French authorities, not least of them the arrangement by which German nationals are employed to teach history to French children. As an additional favor, the French have organized a separate *cours complémentaire*, a post-primary school for children not university-oriented, to relieve the pressure of less capable children in the classroom, which is one of the plagues of the overseas lycée elsewhere. Direction of the school is shared between an administrator detached from the Ministry of Education and a German; and joint staff meetings (always in French) are chaired alternately by the two. But there have been few concessions on questions of program — perhaps inevitably so. As Schneider himself said, "Our problem is this: when little Pierre goes back to France he *must* be able to go to *any* French lycée."

FROM THE CLASSROOM

At the Französischer Gymnasium in Berlin, Dr. Babin, a German teacher of Latin, Greek and history, is working with a class of 12-year-old French and 14-year-old Germans on questions of ancient history. His text is one of Hachette's finest efforts, *L'Orient et la Grèce*, revised in 1964 from the Collection Isaac. Like any really first-rate history teacher, Dr. Babin is teaching not only history but language, frame of reference, art, political science. In this lesson, the emphasis is on political science. For a man like Dr. Babin, a Social Democratic intellectual in his fifties, who was a grown man in the Hitler era and spent his share of time in concentration camps, there is a particular poignancy in teaching the forms of government to the ignorant young. We are in fourth-century Athens:

"Who controls the law?"

A German boy: "The tribunes."

"Who controls the tribunes?"

A French girl, chewing gum: "The assembly of the people."

"Who controls the assembly of the people?" This one gives the students trouble, and Dr. Babin tells them: "The law." But he reminds them also of what Lenin said about the irrelevance of law when the people are stirred. Socrates was killed by the democracy of the town meeting. How is modern democracy different in its operations? The political parties, for example. "If you don't like a law, you can go to your political party and ask them to go to parliament, which can change the law...."

The book refers briefly to the importance of disease in the erosion of the Greek city-states. Dr. Babin sneezes: "*La peste,*" he says. "Why does the plague demoralize people? Because everyone thinks, I will be dead tomorrow. There are the dead bodies in the street, even the vultures won't eat them; there is the stink and the thirst. It is not unlike what we lived through, under Hitler."

4

A third pattern can be found in the French Lycée of London, a school of almost 2,400 students, two-thirds of them English, about a tenth of them from a mixture of 40-odd nationalities, the rest French. As in Rome, the English nationals start at pre-kindergarden level. Many teachers in the early grades speak no English, and children will be admitted above the kindergarten only if they can demonstrate complete fluency in French. "From the age of seven," said Augustin Gaudin while *proviseur* of this lycée, "our teachers go on with their work as though they were in a village school in France. They forget the children are English."

Fees are high by European standards — $700 a year in 1966 — but there is no shortage of applicants. Indeed, after warning that students can be admitted only at age five or earlier, the official brochure of the school in 1965 added, "Children should be registered as early as possible for the Jardin d'Enfants, but registrations are suspended until 1966, the waiting lists at present being much too long."

In theory, all students are taught together, regardless of nationality, up to the age of 15. In fact, the French nationals are segregated out for instruction in French language and literature from an earlier age, and instruction in English by English teachers begins in mathematics and science from age 14, for students planning to take O-level G.C.E. examinations. While the French and other foreigners in Rome are taught Italian by French teachers — and nobody in the Rome lycée is permitted to offer Italian as a first foreign language on the *baccalauréat* — the London lycée does employ English teachers to teach English in the English way to all, and permits all candidates for the *bac* to offer English as the first foreign language. (Yet a third system exists in Vienna, where Austrian teachers teach German to Austrian students, who are given grades on the *bac* in German as a foreign language by reference to the grades they have received from their teachers, without any external examination whatever.) But few English students do want the *bac*, which many British universities do not accept as a basic credential; and from the age of 15 the English children study most subjects separately in preparation for their G.C.E.s.

Of the staff of 200 in 1966, about 180 were French nationals; 140 of these were employees of the French government. The rest are wives of Englishmen: "Fortunately for us," said Gaudin, "Paris is near, and Englishmen are eclectic." Three *professeurs agrégés* in mathematics, probably more than can be claimed by any other French lycée outside Paris itself, have been made available to the London lycée via the marriage ceremony. One of them, Mme Denise Ollivera, teaches the *Mathématiques-Elémentaires* program to the final year of the French side, in French; and the A-level mathematics program to the final year of the English side, in English — a remarkable feat of pedagogic virtuosity.

FROM THE CLASSROOM

At the French Lycée of London, Mme Claire Rossano is teaching English to French students 16 and 17 years of age, recently arrived in England to help flesh out the second cycle on the French side, at the ages when most native students are working for the General Certificate of Education. Mme Rossano is a businesslike young lady, and she expects a great deal from her class. Unlike the teacher of Italian in the lycée in Rome, she is a native speaker of English — "the perfect teacher for this class," said Anthony Morgan, who as director of the English side of the school has responsibility for the English taught to French students. "She is the daughter of an English father and a French mother, and had all her schooling here at this lycée. So her approach is basically French." Even the text, for a wonder, is non-French: it is *The English We Use*, by R. A. Close, dedicated to "the many teachers and students of English to whose questions I could only answer, 'This is the English we use.'"

The class has been reading *Wuthering Heights*, and Mme Rossano catechizes the 26 students, one at a time: "What is the strange revelation that Catherine makes in chapter nine? ... Who unfortunately overhears part of this confession, and what part is overheard? ... What is the result, the consequence? ... What other

The French Foreign Lycées

important events take place at the end of this chapter involving Edgar, Catherine and Mrs. Dean?"

We move on to vocabulary questions: "What are the two meanings of 'to halt'?" A girl says, "To stop and to hesitate." Mme Rossano requests three synonyms for "to saunter." Another girl offers "to wander, to stroll, to roam." Mme Rossano asks a boy to use "at a pinch" in a sentence, and he does. "What are the four different parts of the theatre?" A girl answers, "The stalls, the circle, the upper circle, the gallery." Teacher wants an antonym for "to whet, as a knife" — and gets "to blunt."

These children were living in France and studying in French schools the year before, and their accents show it; but their performance is astonishing. Roger Houdret, the new *proviseur* of the lycée, without taking any credit away from Mme Rossano, feels that the greatest single help is television.

5

In South America, an antique but still flourishing nationalism raises other obstacles to the passage of French education through the minds of foreigners. At the Lycée Francais de Montevideo, a mostly Uruguayan staff has accepted the impossible challenge of preparing all its most able students for both the *baccalauréat* and the local *bachillerato*. Moreover, this challenge must be met for the 300 foreign students (about 140 of them French) as well as for the 1,300 Uruguayans. The lycée is a private school, but it must operate under Uruguayan law, and that law requires a minimum number of hours of study of Uruguayan subjects in the Spanish language, by all children in all schools. The eight or ten teachers sent by the French government may not work in Montevideo until the Uruguayan government grants them diplomas equivalent to those required of Uruguayan teachers. The administrative staff sent from France must be individually accepted by the director of secondary education in the Uruguayan ministry.

Fortunately, the required half-day of Spanish does not begin until age 6, so the lycée can teach entirely in French for the three years of the Jardin d'Enfants. At the end of that period a "psycho-pedagogical examination" is given for admission to the primary grades. Then for five years, in large classes (40 or more), the children work both the French and the Uruguayan elementary program. Their teachers in French are mostly graduates of this lycée, which has been in existence since 1922; and it is odd for the visitor (but not for them) to hear them exuding a sophisticated enthusiasm for the delights of a Paris they have never seen. The double program is given to the students in these grades by sheer force-feeding. "In an elementary school of 25 hours a week," said André Thévenin, the *censeur* and theoretician of the school, "we must do what is done in thirty hours in France and in twenty hours in Uruguay."

Organizational differences between the two systems first rear their head in the sixth year, which is for the French the first year of secondary education and for the Uruguayans the last year of primary education. Emphasis must be given here to the Spanish program, because at the end of this year the Uruguayan students must pass the Spanish-language state examination required of all private-school students who wish to proceed to any secondary school, private or public. (At this point, in the words of P. B. Stoyle, who tries to run a similar binational program at the British School of Montevideo, "the rot of the English sets in.") Fortunately, the children are now in the full lycée timetable of 41 hours of class work a week, so their French can be kept going. Though the school is not selective at entrance and lets most children through its "psycho-pedagogical examination" — and though attrition from the first through the sixth year is only from about 150 to about 100 students a grade — 95% of the children pass the Uruguayan examination in a normal year.

"One cannot impose on the future candidates for two Bac-

The French Foreign Lycées

calaureates," Thévenin has written, "an excessive schedule corresponding to the arithmetic sum of the hours in Spanish and the hours in French."[1] Since it is legally impossible to reduce the number of hours in Spanish required at a Uruguayan lycée, the compromise is to teach all students art, music and English with Spanish as the language of control; and mathematics, physics and chemistry in both French and Spanish, with a single bilingual teacher operating in both languages, employing the more difficult French program and texts.

Even so, students cannot prepare for both the French and the Spanish baccalaureates in the same year, and the lycée has taken the heroic step of abandoning completely the final year of the first cycle of French secondary education. With the third year suppressed, students come to the French *bac* a year early, and can devote their last year in school entirely to the Uruguayan examinations, with instruction almost entirely in Spanish. Despite the missing year, 40% to 50% of the children who attempt the French *baccalauréat* succeed on it, which is about the proportion of passes in metropolitan France. Nearly all of those who take the *bachillerato* are pronounced qualified for university.

By then, however, the numbers in the academic program have shrunk considerably. At age 11, the school is streamed on the French side into a group which will work primarily in Spanish with special attention to French as a foreign language; a group which will proceed along the lines of the French "technical college" commercial course; and a group in the standard lycée program. Only about a third of those who proceed to the secondary level of the lycée will in fact attempt the French *baccalauréat*.

---

[1] "Un Enseignement Fondé sur le Bilinguisme: Le Lycée Français de Montevideo," *Le Français dans le Monde*, Vol. 33, June 1965.

That third, on consideration, is a large proportion. Few of the Uruguayan students who struggle so with the two full programs will have any use whatever for their French diploma. It is a meaningless piece of paper in their home country, and not one in fifty of them can hope to go to university in Europe, which is six thousand miles away and offers no travel scholarships to Uruguayans. Indeed, as a practical matter the *baccalauréat* has come to serve a function that could scarcely please de Gaulle if he knew about it. American universities, looking to give scholarships to Uruguayan students, feel an extra degree of confidence in the doubly bachelored product of the lycée. In an average year, none or one of the new graduates will go off to a French university, but half a dozen will continue their education in the United States.

Related, less official but perhaps more intractable difficulties dog the Lycée Pasteur in São Paulo, which goes back to the 1920s and has boomed with this astonishing city in the last dozen years. The arrangements now in effect are necessarily post-war, because Brazil in 1942 — to fight back against Hitler's *Kulturkampf* and nationalize the large numbers of Japanese immigrants — prohibited instruction in languages other than Portuguese. When the law was relaxed in the 1950s, the former German school remained Portuguese in language, but the lycée returned to French. The influence of the local French community, which sends 500 children, is greater at this school than at any other large overseas lycée. A new building for the French program, opened in 1964, was financed entirely by French industry in Brazil, and the French government sends only 11 of the 50 teachers who work in the French program. (The rest are recruited and paid by the school itself.) Thus the school is in constant tension: "What interests the local French community," said René Lejeune, the lycée's *proviseur* in 1965, sitting in an office dominated by two huge, brilliantly colored and fully strung bows made by Brazilian Indians, "is a school just like France. What interests the Foreign Ministry is influence on the local population."

This lycée is split into two entirely separate schools, housed in buildings half a dozen miles apart in São Paulo's impenetrable urban sprawl. The old building educates almost 2,300 Brazilians, studying in Portuguese, with special attention to French as a foreign language. The new building takes about 1,050, of whom about 950 are in the *baccalauréat* and 100 in the Brazilian "classical" program, which has enough in common with the *bac* to be taught here rather than there. Some 140 students of Brazilian nationality are in the French *bac* program, under the conditions of a Franco-Brazilian treaty which grants partial recognition to the French document; these students have to take examinations in Portuguese before they can proceed to Brazilian universities. Nearly all of them do. The failure rate nationally on the Brazilian *vestibular* is almost 60%, but it is a matter of deep concern at the lycée when one of the French-program students fails. The 300 students in the *bac* program who are neither French nor Brazilian are drawn from 28 nationalities; about a dozen of them are Americans, despite the presence in São Paulo of a large and ambitious American school.

Both Portuguese and English are required every year from students in the *baccalauréat* course; otherwise the program is that of the metropolitan lycée. Most students are a little older than their counterparts in France: because the school year runs from April to December, students transferring from the Northern Hemisphere must either advance or retreat a school year, and most are told to retreat.

Because French industry picks up the bills and most of the teachers must be recruited privately, the staff is more international than that at most lycées. Eight nationalities are represented, with a number of Egyptians, Swiss and Belgians. The last-year *Mathématiques-Elémentaires* course is taught by an Israeli national who did his graduate work at the University of Beirut in happier times. Few of the teachers at the French branch are Brazilian, because by law Brazilian teachers must teach at more than one school. The *proviseur* estimated that most Brazilian teachers work 70 hours a week, teaching morning, afternoon and night classes in three different establishments, to earn a very minimal living wage. The non-Brazilian staff in the secondary school teaches a maximum of 18 hours a week, and is forbidden to hold outside jobs.

Another aspect of the Lycée Pasteur should be noted — the extraordinary sweetness of the atmosphere, the love across generations which came from responsibilities accepted on both sides, and which is by no means so uncommon in French schools as myth-makers and movie-makers insist. Lejeune, with eight children of his own, gravely shook hands in the halls with the children he passed, and called them by name. An outgrowth of this atmosphere was social service work by students and staff — and especially by Mme Lejeune, who is a physician — in the *favela* which stands in a valley below the school. Ten thousand people live in this little valley, housed in shacks, dependent on two pumps for their entire water supply. Lejeune considered it part of the education of his students, a necessary adjunct to the religion courses, that the older children go down to the *favela* and do whatever they could to help.

One more South American school and then cry, Hold enough: the lycée of Buenos Aires. Here there are no governmental problems: a Franco-Argentinian treaty gives the secondary school full powers to teach an exclusively French program and accepts the *baccalauréat* as documentation equal to

The French Foreign Lycées

the local *bachillerato* for university entrance. Some time before 1970, the situation in Buenos Aires will be precisely to the French taste, like that of Rome: during his visit to Argentina in 1965, de Gaulle signed the papers for the construction of an official French state lycée to be built on land given for the purpose by the Argentine government. At this writing, however, the French lycée of Buenos Aires is still a private proprietary school, which has been for three decades the property and the living of M. Crespin, its director, an amiably blunt man with a Rotary pin in his buttonhole. "I am," he said in 1965, "the only French lycée where I am the *maître*." A twist of the knife — something Crespin does not mention but the French Ministry of Foreign Affairs does — comes with the fact that Crespin himself is not French but Belgian.

The lycée has about 1,500 students beyond the Jardin d'Enfants, which is separately established. Almost 600 students are French, many of them dependents of the big Renault factory in the city; about 750 are Argentinian; and the other 150 are "international." Spanish is taught, Crespin said, "as it would be in France — with emphasis on Spanish, not South American culture and literature." The other foreign language taught is English. "Those who go to the United States to university," said Crespin rather airily, "to Harvard, Columbia, California, Stanford, find that they speak well after only a few months." Staffing this course is not easy, however, because people who are thoroughly bilingual in English and French (the language of control) are hard to find in Spanish-speaking countries. For some years Crespin employed an English lady; in 1965, both the teachers of English were of Polish nationality.

Inevitably, Crespin's lycée must live off the private Argentinian economy. In theory, his primary school, which offers half a day in French and half a day on the Argentinian program in Spanish, should be entitled to an 80% subsidy from the Argentine government; but "they don't pay it." Classes are large, up to 50; all rooms are crowded with seats, and all seats are occupied. The vast majority of the teachers are Argentinians (of French descent, Crespin noted); many took their secondary education in this school. "It is a question of the spirit of the house," Crespin said in 1965. "After 31 years, we know what we are doing." But the Argentinian teacher, like his Brazilian colleague, must hold more than one job, and the atmosphere at the Buenos Aires lycée was one of rush and bustle.

Even to this wholly private school, the French government sends teachers — only five of them to be sure, but an important five, including the mathematics, physics and chemistry teachers. French flexibility can go even further. The Istanbul lycée, a Turkish state school, draws half its staff from France at the expense of the French. A new French school starting up in Japan is run by Carthusian monks — but will receive French government support. Everything is possible, provided the language is French.

CHAPTER 7: **American Overseas Schools**

Apart from the French, no nation has a tradition of exporting its culture through schools. Where Britain had an Empire the taste for out-of-date British educational practice, like the taste for cricket and tea, survives political change; and British schools, sporadically supported by the British Council, survive in centers of expatriate British population like Rome and Florence, at occasional entrepôts like Hamburg, and in those parts of South America where the railroads were built with British capital. Rarely are they a major factor on the secondary level. The British habit of sending children to boarding schools for the secondary years, particularly ingrained in the social class most likely to be found abroad, prevented the construction of significant systems of English foreign schools for adolescents even during the heyday of English influence. After World War II and the post-war currency restrictions, there was little or no British community in many of the places which had once sustained English schools. Where such schools are still in business, especially in South America, they tend to live both financially and educationally on the local economy, serving a local population largely in the local language, with English as a specially emphasized first foreign language. Their teachers tend to be very young, highly transient and atrociously underpaid.

Nor can it be said that the American schools export American culture. American high culture is scarcely exported at all, and the low culture is far more efficiently and pervasively transported by the movie and television producers, the soap-and-toothpaste makers and the advertising agencies. But even apart from the military dependents' schools and the schools which are branches of oil and mining companies, some 250 or so American schools overseas in 1967 probably enrolled more than 75,000 children. In those countries where the official language is neither English nor French, the American overseas schools probably educate more children than the French foreign lycée system.

American schools scatter the length of South America, in towns as well as in big cities, dot the map of Europe, and function in all Asian countries where the Agency for International Development is active, from Iran and Afghanistan to Thailand and Korea. With few exceptions, their population is predominantly American (in most Asian countries, local children are not permitted to attend schools operated by foreigners). But a few American schools (most notably the one in Guatemala City) are designed, like the French lycée, to serve a largely local population; and most of them will welcome the children of the other foreigners in town. In places like Frankfurt and Vienna, more than a third of the students are "international." One of these establishments, Berlin's John F. Kennedy School, is fully binational, part of the Berlin city school system but operated conjointly with a committee of resident Americans headed ex officio by the chief of the U. S. Information Service.

Nearly all American schools abroad are the creation and the creature of the parent community. Describing the situation of American children in Asia in the early 1960s, Elizabeth Bole Eddison wrote: "No single agency or group was taking any responsibility for their education. Whether these children were educated well or badly depended (and still depends) largely on the parents who were at a certain place at a certain time. . . . If these parents were knowledgeable or interested or determined, things were apt to go reasonably well. If the parents felt it didn't matter or that everything was up to the school, then things went badly or not at all."[1]

As a result, American schools suffer from a lack of that professionalism which characterizes the lycée and from the tides of sentiment which inevitably flow from the fact that, as one principal put it, "the parent whose child is doing well thinks it's a good school and the parent whose child is doing badly thinks it's a bad school." There is also a fearful lack of continuity in the leadership of most of these schools as significant members of the board are rotated around the world by their employers.

By no stretch of the imagination can these American schools be considered part of a "system." All have sprung up independently and each is a law unto itself. The teachers do not consider themselves part of a separate corps, elite or otherwise. Because teachers' salaries in the United States are by far the highest in the world and because all these schools are almost entirely dependent on tuition payments for their revenues, the staff consists of people who could be making more money from their work if they had not gone abroad. Unlike the

[1] "American Schools Overseas," *Vassar Alumnae Magazine*, June 1965.

French teachers, the Americans must also sacrifice career standing and privileges on going abroad: they lose their pension rights and their seniority where they have been teaching.

American overseas schools have some access to teachers taking a sabbatical leave abroad and to the American wives of local nationals or of diplomats, technicians and executives assigned abroad. In recent years a few schools have negotiated formal arrangements with a stateside system by which, for example, Bucks County, Pa., supplies one or two teachers a year on a rotating basis to the American school in São Paulo. But by and large the schools must draw their staff from young people moving into the profession, and from remittance men (and ladies) who find they need a little more money to continue living in, say, Rome.

A few of the functions of the French governmental apparatus are performed by a private non-profit organization in New York, International Schools Services. This institution, which has an odd and interesting history, was founded by accident out of Geneva's International Schools Association, which needed a fund-raising operation in America. Russell Cook, an officer of the International Telecommunications Union who is president of I.S.A., took the problem to Arthur Sweetser in retirement in Washington, and persuaded him to accept the chairmanship of a body to be called the International Schools Foundation. The foundation put out a pamphlet called "New Links" and settled into quiescence.

Meanwhile, the headmaster of New York's New Lincoln School, John Brooks, had resigned his job and gone traveling around the world for a year. He visited the schools which served American children wherever he went — "in the great trackless waste where to put your child in a local school is really to be nuts" — and he was shocked by their physical and pedagogical condition. On his return, he went to the Ford

Foundation, whose officers agreed he had found a need Ford could meet but pointed out that they were not in the habit of giving grants to individuals. Someone at Ford knew about the inactive shell of the International Schools Foundation, and Brooks was sent off to see Sweetser and, if Sweetser agreed, to take over I.S.F. Sweetser did agree and Ford made a grant.

International Schools Services is a charity, not a membership organization: its services are available without charge to any school abroad which accepts American children. It will advertise for, interview and screen applicants for teaching or administrative jobs, and it offers curriculum guides and suggestions for financial and corporate management. These services have been paid for by contributions and foundation grants, but in recent years other sources of income have become necessary. A little money has been raised by organizing "Councils of International Schools" in different regions, membership groups which could take over the financing of some of the I.S.S. work, but this effort has been hard to sustain, partly because the schools all have their own financial troubles and partly because it is always difficult to persuade people to pay for things they are accustomed to receiving free.

Since 1964, I.S.S. has had annual subventions from the U. S. State Department, out of the few hundred thousand dollars for schools in South America which Congress has appropriated every year, more or less routinely, since Franklin Roosevelt became concerned about the German-language schools Hitler was founding in an attempt to seduce America's Good Neighbors. Another source of revenue for I.S.S. has been industry with international commitments, especially oil and mining companies which contract with the organization to establish and distantly supervise schools, taking an override on the budget for its work. (These projects take much of the time of Brooks' successor, John Sly, a young Harvard-trained teacher and administrator who came to I.S.S. from a decade in Africa, where he ran schools for local governments as well as for foreign industries.) To most American schools abroad, however, I.S.S. is simply a source of free recruitment help, advice and moral support.

Some federal money has been available to private, non-profit, non-sectarian American schools abroad under the terms of the Smith-Mundt Act of 1948 and under Public Law 480, which establishes guidelines for the disposal of the "counterpart funds" in local currency which countries receiving surplus American agricultural produce have been required to set aside. These laws are administered by a small Office of Overseas Schools in the State Department, which investigates applications for aid from existing schools and every so often, sub rosa, helps a group get a school started. The basic criteria are that the school "must meet a demonstrated need for American-type educational facilities in the community or region"; that it must be acceptable to the local government; that the board must at least contain representation of resident Americans (preferably including people from the embassy or consulate), and the director "wherever practicable, should be a U. S. citizen"; that "the curriculum and instruction should . . . reflect accepted U. S. theory and practice in education"; and that "the peoples of the host country or other countries" should be enrolled in the school.

Interpretations of these criteria have varied widely from time to time and from place to place — at The Hague, for example, a first application for construction funds was turned down because the director (Jan Van Der Valk) was a Dutch rather than a U. S. national; and a second application was turned down because there were no Dutch children in the school; but a third application was approved, provided that the building were planned and used for all four national divisions of the school and not just the American division. Generally, U. S. government money has not been available for operating expenses, and the State Department will not help schools recruit teachers or plan programs. The most usual grants are for buildings and for scholarships to local students. Otherwise, the American schools overseas must subsist on the revenues available from tuition and on the wits of the people on the scene. "If you go find money from American corporations," said Robert Ianuzelli, assistant head of the American School of Madrid in 1967, "you have the problem of offering the school to all their employees. You must now draw up at least one course *everybody* can get through."

Historically, the French lycée and the English "public" school functioned as entities relatively independent of the community immediately surrounding them. Artificially nurtured and promoting a national rather than a local purpose, such schools could adapt without strain to changed surroundings. But the American school is in design an organism of its environment, responsive at all times to its local community. Abroad, this community lacks definition, and to retain the nurture of its roots the American school stretched an umbilical cord back to an assumed mother country, the general suburban culture of upper-middle-class United States. Whatever facet of the American overseas school is examined, the observer finds himself drawn into a central unanswered question: what is the purpose of the institution? Founded in and sustained by transient need, can it without deliberate governmental direction become more than a public convenience?

FROM
THE CLASSROOM

In one of the gleaming new science laboratories at the American Overseas School of Rome (from which the descriptive word "international" was stripped in 1964), a white-haired lady with a soft

Scotch accent is supervising the work of a class of 15-year-olds in the laboratory manual of "blue book" Biological Sciences Curriculum Study — the most theoretical, most chemical and in the general view most difficult of the three B.S.C.S. biology courses. "We can't get okra seeds," she says a little fretfully, walking about the room with the visitor. "So we're trying experiments with other vegetables and reporting back to B.S.C.S." She calls a girl away from a sink to describe what's going on. The girl says, "We're set up in five groups of three people each, each has its own responsibilities. The lab assistants' group meets after school and learns techniques. For instance, we had to dissect frogs to get the eggs and raise the tads in a hormone solution." The teacher breaks in: "We've had a little trouble with Italian frogs." The girl continues: "It's a fantastic experience, really, having to care for them, making your own solution, doing your own experiment, finding your own results."

The ninth-graders enter the room, carrying *Silas Marner* and *Idylls of the King*. On the wall is a card headed *Sistema Periodica Degli Elementi*, looking just like any other wall card of Mendelejeff's table, but, still . . .

2

The American School of Paris was founded in 1945 by employees of the American Embassy. Its first home was a pair of rooms in the American Church, and its first staff was volunteer, mostly wives of Embassy personnel. At the end of the first year they hired Paul DeRosay, who had run a school in Paris before the war, and moved to the Students' and Artists' Club in the American Cathedral. "This was no problem," said Douglas McKee, literary agent and English teacher, who has been associated with the school since 1947 and served as its acting headmaster in 1964–65. "There were no students and artists in 1947. But then someone died, and left the Students' and Artists' Club twenty-five thousand dollars, and the will was attacked on the grounds that the place was no longer a Students' and Artists' Club but a school. So the school got thirty days' notice to get out, and they dumped our furniture in the courtyard. We found a house to rent in Boulogne, then a bigger house for the high school. But people were concerned, and said, 'You need your own place.' "

Among the properties on the Paris real estate market at this time was Coty's reconstruction of Mme Du Barry's love nest, on the cliffs above the Seine at Louveciennes. Though the house itself was as genuine as a three-dollar bill, the grounds were planted as Du Barry had planted them, and were classified as historic property, which meant that any purchaser would have to accept an obligation to keep the gardens as they were. Nevertheless, the school bought this house and the four acres around it, plus five acres across the road. Until 1967–68, the high school was housed in the old love nest reconstruction, classrooms in the eighteenth-century-style gimcrackery on the ground floor and in the servants' quarters upstairs. The junior high was in the mansion that came with the adjacent property, and the elementary school in temporary buildings on the adjacent grounds. Plans had been filed for the construction of something more permanent for the little ones, but it developed that there were once quarries below the cliff, and before any new substantial structure could be added the quarries would have to be filled with concrete, at a cost estimated at $150,000. This was not the only problem. The road that separates the two properties does not belong to the town but to the Ministry of Fine Arts, because it services a machine at the foot of the cliff which pumps the water for the fountains of Versailles. "And the man at the machine hated us," said McKee, "because our school buses blocked his trucks." In 1967 the school gave up on Louveciennes, and moved to quarters newly vacated by NATO in Saint-Cloud.

There were about 700 students at the school, 90% of them American nationals, the rest mixed. A dozen French children attended on a one-year basis, their tuition paid by scholarship grant from the U.S. State Department. The teachers of French were native speakers of the language, and there were half a dozen English (including a former mathematics teacher at Gordonstoun), but the great majority of the staff of 60 was American. Grants from the State Department paid the salaries of one teacher each in science, mathematics and social studies. Salaries in 1965 started at $3,700 a year for new American teachers and $2,300 for new European teachers; but there was no trouble staffing the school, because people want to live in Paris. For two staff vacancies in the 1965–66 academic year, the American School of Paris had 800 applicants. (One of the vacancies was caused by the departure of a Spanish teacher formerly of the University of Madrid. "He was used to teaching serious university students," McKee commented, "not girls thinking of dates.")

The program is that of a good up-to-date American suburban school, with new math and new science, giant reading lists in English, and a humanities course. French is compulsory for all except those who enter in the last two years with no French but at least two years of another language: they can continue what they began. A charming unit in the social studies program sent "the brighter half of the ninth grade" out to interview the candidates and voters in the municipal election of Louveciennes and to make a report (with the mayor and the *proviseur* of the local lycée in attendance) on how city government works in a Paris suburb. The emphasis, necessarily, is on preparation for college; and a number of Advanced Placement courses are offered. Both staff and students are unusually stable for an international school: staff turnover is rarely as much as ten per cent a year, and the average student spends four years at the school. A couple of years ago the basketball team was champion of the "lycée league" for all France. The board would like to have more students who are not Americans. But, of course, neither its diploma nor the College Boards, which are all the school can prepare students for, are accepted by universities outside the United States and Canada.

Very similar results have been achieved from a different beginning at the American School of Brussels, originally a joint Anglo-American venture of the days shortly after World War II. After some initial flounderings, the school in 1951 found Arthur Denyer, an Englishman who had been a county Chief Education Officer before the war and had served in the British Army as an educational administrator. His wife was a Belgian lawyer, and after the war he settled in Brussels, where, "being very clever — you know, fly — I took to importing British gas stoves to Belgium and went broke. I looked for a job in Belgium, and the American Embassy came through with an FS-9 job as a bookkeeper. I had no clearance, so they gave me no work; and I set up a Coke machine and an ice-cream bar in the office, made a few hundred dollars a month from it. When the clearance came through, it showed 'schoolmaster.' Colonel Murphy at the Embassy said, instead of doing bookkeeping, why don't you run our school?" When Denyer took over in 1951 the school had 37 pupils; in 1965, when he left, it had 660, and it was no longer Anglo-American. More than 90% of the children were of U. S. nationality; of the 200-odd in the high school, only five or six were anything else.

Like most American overseas schools, the American School of Brussels sits well out from the city and the children come on buses. The central building is a chateau with a couple of new rooms built onto it to lift student capacity to about 250. Two wooden one-story classroom buildings were contributed by the city of Brussels in return for the right to use the property for underprivileged children during the summer (and for overflow visitors during the 1958 World's Fair). A new, more solid, two-story library-and-classroom building was put up with contributions from American industry.

Most of the children at the Brussels school were from business families, where the father worked for a company securing its foothold in the Common Market. The staff was not happy about their attitudes. "These people," said one of Denyer's assistants, "have domestic help for the first time. They have to have a cocktail party with three drinks every night, and they forget their kids are in a foreign country and lost. That's our worst problem — if we could do something about *that*, we could handle everything else." To add insult to injury, Denyer said, "American businessmen aren't used to paying school fees." Including transportation and lunch, fees in 1965 ran about $900 a year, $750 of it for schooling. The staff was overwhelmingly British, save for the native French speakers who taught French and a handful of American wives of medical students at the University of Louvain. Turnover of children was rapid: "There are virtually no children here now," Denyer said, "who were here three years ago." But the staff was stable, with a number of teachers who had been at the school eight or ten years. Salary in 1965 was at the British scale plus about $1,500 a year "living allowance."

For one brief moment in 1960, the Brussels school seemed destined to be a fully international school. Negotiations to affiliate it with the Scholae Europaeae had been almost completed, approved by the chief of Her Majesty's Inspectors, the Belgian Ministry of Education, Denyer, and van Houtte for the European Schools — when de Gaulle ruled Britain out of the Common Market. By the autumn of 1965, when Denyer left, internationalism no longer seemed a major objective. "I'm running an American school, not an international school," said Donald Phillips, Denyer's successor. "I need an operating subsidy for staff and a capital subsidy for buildings to do the kind of job that would be done in a reasonably good suburban high school — and to get that degree of diversification which would enable us to meet the board's directive that the school shall not be selective."

FROM
THE CLASSROOM

At the American School of Paris, Richard Baugh, an Englishman, is working with an all-U. S. class on the problems of what used to be called intermediate algebra — except that his text is Richardson's *College Algebra* and his approach is "modern" beyond the ambitions of most American teachers who say they teach modern math.

The problem on the board is $y < x, y > x^2$. The solution to this is that both x and y are fractions, but the method of showing it is what counts. The inequality $y < x$ can be represented on a graph by a shaded area below the diagonal; the inequality $y > x^2$ is the area inside a parabola. The area inside both (the "set" of points on the graph) is the solution to the pair of inequalities. "Shade it in," Baugh urges, walking around the room and looking at the graphs his charges are drawing. "That's the only way you can do these things. Draw it carefully, shade it in, see if you can guess how big that area should be, hmm?" One student who is not with it asks, "Should it be bigger than three?" Baugh says, cryptically, "You know, one-half times one-half — don't you?"

Then he writes on the board a specific problem:

$$xy < 4$$
$$x + y < 8$$
$$x > 0$$
$$y > 0$$

"Give me that in one minute." Only three or four of the class of twenty get it, and for the rest he draws it on the board — the positive quarter of the graph, a diagonal from 8 on the y axis to 8 on the x axis, and the curved line of xy = 4, which slices through the shaded area. A girl says, "xy equals four is a hyperbola," and he picks it up. He ends the unit hopefully with the comment, "You see, any inequality gives you a shading."

3

Paris and Brussels are typical of American schools abroad in organization and purposes. A less common, and somewhat more interesting, situation is that of the American International School of Frankfurt, founded in 1960 by a group of parents and businessmen with the help of Jack Harrison, a casually energetic young man from San Diego who had been assistant in charge of the American wing at the NATO lycée in Saint-Germain-en-Laye. "The basic difference between our operation and that of other international schools," Harrison said shortly before he resigned as director in 1965, "is the cooperation of the German authorities, from the head of the Frankfurt school system to the Ministry of Culture. We are a German school. We teach in English, but we are recognized as a German private school." In 1966 the Ministry formally approved the American International School of Frankfurt as part of the area's educational facility, and extended a subvention of $200 a pupil, regardless of nationality.

Frankfurt had about 600 students in 1965, roughly 330 of them American nationals, 75 each German and British, 30-odd Israeli and Canadian, the rest from all over. "There are two American schools here," Harrison said. "If you're working for a business, you can send your child to the military school for a tuition about $200 a year less than ours. So we can screen. And if we have a choice between a Britisher and an American, we'll usually take the one who has no other place to go."

The program at the Frankfurt school includes compulsory

German and French from first grade. There are reception classes for non-English-speaking children at all levels, and intensive work in German is given to those who arrive without that language. The school also has a course in "German for Germans — and there are more non-Germans in it than Germans. Perhaps it's not quite up to *Abitur* standards, it's only one hour a day, but we hope." In the ninth and tenth grades, a required course in world history is taught in both German and English, though this innovation was unpopular when it was launched in 1964. "Forty per cent of our ninth- and tenth-graders are fluent enough in German," Harrison said, "but they're the ones who want to be more American than anyone else."

By the terms of its arrangements with the local Ministry of Education, the Frankfurt school has obliged itself to offer a thirteenth year, to prepare some kind of *Abitur* or an international examination if one is approved. The first graduating class from twelfth grade, however, was not achieved until 1967, and on Harrison's departure the new regime decided to concentrate its energies on improving service to transient Americans. Six of the twelve teachers who had founded the school remained for Harrison's four years, but all left at the end of that time, as did several British teachers, seduced away to preparatory schools in the United States. "Parents went home and spread the word," Harrison said. "And the salaries in the United States are so much higher...."

Despite the unattractiveness of the city, the Frankfurt school's teacher recruitment position has been good because its salaries are the best in Europe. In 1966–67 the school paid about $5,100 a year to beginning teachers, plus an annual travel allowance of $300. The higher salaries were paid despite maximum class sizes of about 20 in the high school and 16 in the elementary school, and despite relatively low tuition charges (about $600 a year), in part through the German subvention and in larger part through budgetary policy. "Most international schools," Harrison said, "budget on American public school percentage for teachers [i.e., about three-fifths is allocated to salaries]. We pay considerably more and have no difficulty operating on our income. There's a great temptation to spend operating funds for things like slate blackboards. We won't do it. We don't have a slate blackboard in the school, and when we buy one it will be out of the proceeds of a capital-funds drive." Thanks to the German-American cultural exchange program, American teachers in Germany need not pay taxes to the Germans on their first two years' salary. Though this arrangement inevitably promotes two-year turnover, Harrison felt the merry-go-round could be avoided, for the people the school really wanted to keep, through "career salary schedules."

4

Recognition agreements like the one in Frankfurt are a matter of law rather than choice for the American schools in South America, where schools and teachers must be approved by the ministries of education whether or not they accept local students. At least half the teachers in the elementary grades in Brazil must be Brazilian nationals, and half the day, more or less, must be taught in Portuguese. On the secondary level, these restrictions are usually less severe; but the schools, having accepted local children for the bilingual program in the early grades, will usually make a greater effort to take care of their special needs in high school.

At the American School of Rio de Janeiro, for example, about a third of the students are from families where English is not spoken at home, and most of this group are Brazilian.

The school sits behind the beach at Leblon, round the mountain from Copacabana. Its courtyard during recess is almost as noisily unrestrained (and almost as alive with soccer balls) as that at any European school. Five years of advanced Portuguese are offered, as are history and geography courses taught in the local language. Brazilian students add courses which make their program similar to that at the Pedro II School in town; and on graduation they take the Pedro II examinations, which will admit them to the examinations given by the faculties at the local universities.

At the Escola Graduada in São Paulo (where the students wear zipper jackets bearing the English legend "Graded"), no fewer than 54 levels of Portuguese are offered every year, and there are 11 Brazilian teachers who teach only Portuguese language in a school of 820 children. The school sent questionnaires to American colleges to ask if Portuguese (for which there is no College Board examination) was acceptable as a second language for entrance, and every college said it was. "Besides," said Stanley S. Beans, principal of the high school, "our kids can take College Boards in Spanish or Italian and do better than kids in the United States who have studied them."

So far, both parts of this argument have been acceptable to the American business community which provides half the students and the entire board of directors (the companies represented in 1966 included du Pont, Ford, Wilson, Swift, Sherwin-Williams, Sears Roebuck and General Electric). About a hundred children are from the many Christian missions to the Brazilian Indian tribes, nearly all of them based in São Paulo; only 35 or so are from U.S. government agencies. Nearly 20% are local children, and 15% are from third countries (Sweden is the most heavily represented, with 22 students in 1966). "We're probably the only *large* American school not in the capital of the country," said Stanley W. Krouse, Jr., director of the school from 1961 through 1966. "Our children are from the executive group in industry, and at this level industry does not send people for just a year or two. A man commits himself here; this is his home."

The Escola Graduada, which dates back to 1922, has been housed since 1961 in a new, handsome, rambling California-style one-story brick school plant out in the barren countryside about fifteen miles from what passes for the center of the city in São Paulo. The school averages about 50 graduates a year, of whom about 40 go on to university, mostly in America, though by hook or crook graduates in the early sixties were accepted at South African, German, Hungarian and Swiss universities. The situation for Brazilian students was still fluid at last report: the Ministry of Education had consented to accept most of the school's program as the equivalent of the program in Brazil's "scientific" high schools, but required additional examinations in Portuguese before granting a school-leaving certificate.

Teacher turnover is fairly heavy — 15% to 20% a year from a staff of about 60 (about 30 U. S. nationals, 20-odd Brazilian nationals, the rest scattered). The program is conservative American, with traditional mathematics and science in the secondary school, except for a superb and original biology course taught by a former Italian medical missionary who, among other things, takes the children for an annual trip to a hospital to observe the dissection of a cadaver. An extremely capable Frenchman in exile, Roger Allain, teaches four years of French courses, using for the beginners an excellent Hachette direct-method text from 1941. Every year the American schools of Rio, São Paulo and Brasilia join forces for a boat trip up the Amazon for some dozens of high school students.

Where the aim is to educate large numbers of local children

as well as Americans, in the style of the lycée, far greater degrees of acceptance by the host authorities are required. Looking to interest American foundations, Nido de Aguilas (Eagle's Nest), the American school in Santiago de Chile (which had got itself into the hands of local money-lenders on its building program, and was trying to pay $55,000 a year interest on total receipts of about $140,000 a year), a "planning committee" proposed mathematics and science courses to be taught either by pairs of English- and Spanish-speaking teachers or by one bilingual teacher who could teach in a different language every other day. This proposal was not so unrealistic as it may appear, by the way, because one of the American modern mathematics programs (S.M.S.G.) and P.S.S.C. physics had already been translated into Spanish and approved by the Chilean Ministry of Education for use by Chilean students, so that the same textbook could be made available to each child in his own language. The projected enrollment for this school in 1970, in the plans, showed 230 Americans and 420 Chileans, and the inevitable first target of the planners was acceptance of the program by the Chilean Ministry as a means of access to the second-level examinations which grant university entrance.

The importance of the university entrance privilege is demonstrated by the American School of Mexico City, which has as its stated purpose "to prepare qualified students in the English language for entrance into United States colleges and universities" but has been able to maintain its proportion of local students at about one-third, thanks largely to a special accord with the Autonomous National University of Mexico. "The reason we got the accord," said an administrator at the school, "was that the director and sub-director of the University had sent their children to our elementary school." The elementary school is totally bilingual, by Mexican law, and the secondary school runs primarily in English, with supplementary work in Spanish literature and Mexican history (in Spanish) for those on the National University track. (The university also requires a course in philosophy, which is taught, however, in English.) Part of the special accord eliminates the trigonometry requirement otherwise applied to all Mexican university applicants. But two years of biology, a year of chemistry and one of physics are necessary.

Natural selection reduces the proportion of Mexicans in a grade from 60% in kindergarten to 40% in fourth grade, 20% in ninth grade and 10% in the graduating class. The accord with the National University is good only for students who have had the full six years of the school's secondary program, which prevents replacement of those who leave. An additional option is offered to the school's graduates, Mexican or American, by the University of the Americas, a private liberal arts college in Mexico City. Not quite 10% of the graduating class in 1966 was neither American nor Mexican; in all, there were 59 nationalities in the school in late 1965.

The program for bilingual children includes courses in Spanish in contemporary Mexico, history of Spain, literature of Spain, and Latin American literature. For American children arriving at an elementary school age, the school has written its own Spanish materials leading toward bilingualism; but the guidance counselors estimate a year and a half as the average time required before an American child is ready to move into the full bilingual program.

Several American schools exist primarily as a service for the host country. The most admired of them, probably, is the one in Guatemala City, founded in 1945 and largely the creation of Robert MacVean, an athletic former naval officer sent to the country on a diplomatic mission, who fell in love with the place and stayed. Housed on 52 acres of hilltop in superb school buildings designed by a Mexican architect who developed a "shell structure" of concrete hyperbolic roofs and glass walls, the American School of Guatemala City has about 925 students, more than 80% of them Guatemalans, about 15% Americans. Twenty of its sixty teachers are U. S. nationals. After a bilingual elementary school through seventh grade, the organization breaks into separate five-year *bachillerato* and high school programs, with relatively little interchange between the two. The school is licensed by the Minister of Education as an experimental school, and is empowered to excuse students from physics, chemistry and mathematics beyond elementary algebra. "*Officially*," MacVean said, stressing the word, "Guatemalans cannot enter their own universities from the high school program." In fact the Catholic University has always been sympathetic and helpful, and out of the thirteen graduates in 1965 who went through the English-speaking side of the high school, only eight were Americans. In 1966 MacVean started his own American-style college, affiliated with the local Catholic university, to provide an assured home for his graduates and his ideas.

The Guatemala school is subsidized by the American government to the extent of about $10,000 a year for scholarships. The Agency for International Development also provided a grant of $250,000 and low-interest loans of $700,000 to help build the $1.25 million new school. Salaries for teachers in 1966 ranged from $2,300 for a beginner to $4,800 top, which is not enough to draw and keep American teachers; half of the twenty Americans on the staff can be expected to leave every year. Still, the salaries are better than most Guatemalan teachers can expect elsewhere, and the school's basic constituency is the Guatemalan community. A solid majority of American parents in Guatemala City, significantly, prefer their own, all-American Mayan School, which has 300 pupils in a kindergarten-to-ninth grade program, as against MacVean's 125 Americans in a kindergarten-to-twelfth grade program. "The parents who send children to us," MacVean said, "are those who want them to learn Spanish and associate with Guatemalan kids."

Much the same situation has developed in Quito, Ecuador, where the American school relates primarily to the Ecuadorian children, and the expatriate parent community has formed a separate all-American school for its own. The State Department has mixed feelings about such splittings off. According to Ernest N. Mannino, head of the Office of Overseas Schools, "The Department has to be able to say to people being recruited, 'Yes, there is a school for your children. What do you want?' The one thing they always say they want is a school that will allow the boy to go back to tenth grade at home in two years."

FROM
THE CLASSROOM

At the Lincoln American School of Buenos Aires, the elementary classes are in a new building put up with U. S. government money, but the secondary classes are jammed in one way or another into the former private house next door. About 30 of the 230 students in the four-year high school are non-English-speaking, but the only Argentinians are children of people who work in the Foreign Ministry. The Indonesian and Israeli embassies also use this school rather than the French lycée or the British or half-British schools of the area (none of which is sufficiently convenient to the city to permit attendance by day students). In all there are about 20 nationalities represented.

This class is in physics, and its teacher is an Argentine national, Dr. Naum Mittleman, who also teaches chemistry and chemical engineering on the Faculty of Exact Sciences in the University of Buenos Aires. He uses material from several textbooks, and makes up his own course.

"Now," he says, "we don't want to invade the province of the mathematics department, but we must distinguish between an implied and an explicit function. Here we have——" He writes on the blackboard:

$$p = \frac{nRT}{V}$$

A boy breaks in: "Sir, did you hear that Chick just got accepted to Rice?"

Dr. Mittleman congratulates Chick, and calls a boy to the blackboard to work out a problem using the formula. As he starts, Mittleman adds an initial assignment: "Larry, can you prove that specific volume is the reciprocal of density? I give you thirty seconds." Larry, taking about a minute, has the proof on the board, but one of the students doesn't see it. "Will you explain it to Nancy in terms of oranges, please?" Mittleman requests. As the example proceeds, the weight of air at 0° becomes a factor in getting to the volume in the problem, and a boy calls out from his seat, "I understand it now — we never had specific volume before and this was a way to approach it."

"Yes!" Mittleman says with great pleasure. "I never want you to have just one way. I want you to have two, three, more ways, so whether you see it from north, east, south or west it always looks the same." The boy is still working at the board, and as he comes to the penultimate step Mittleman stops him. "We have the privilege now that we are going to face a universal constant, and you are about to miss it. You will meet very few universal constants in your life, and you should know them.

". . . I want you to distinguish carefully between terms which have meaning outside the atomic molecular theory and terms which have meaning only in the frame of the atomic molecular theory.

We must know when we are introducing a parameter. Now *that's* a good word — how many of you know the word parameter? . . ."

5

Other schools, American in inspiration and support, are fundamentally part of the private school system of their host countries. Athens College, for example, a secondary school founded forty years ago by a committee of Greek nationals and Dr. Homer W. Davis, has an entirely Greek pupil population, most from the city, some from Greek families abroad sending the children home. The school was started, Dr. Davis said, "after eleven years of war and revolution, with a million and a half refugees in the country, by a group of Greeks who thought they could influence public education better with a model school than with a committee report. We did very creative work from 1931 to 1938, but then the dictatorship wrecked everything. And the occupation . . . From 1946 to 1950 nothing could be done except day-to-day adjustment to the needs of students who had had no education for four years." Ages at the school range from 9 to 19, and for the first four years English is taught only as a foreign language. After that some courses are taught in English rather than Greek — two years of mathematics, two of geography, three of history and one of psychology. "English-language courses are never as much as half the program," Dr. Davis said.

The faculty of 109 in 1965 included 15 Americans, most of them transients because the school could not pay a living wage. The native English-speaking staff is supplemented by nine "teaching fellows," new graduates of American universities (the program started with only Yale and Princeton, but has now expanded substantially) who trade instruction in Greek and a year in Athens for help with English in the upper grades. The introduction to English is via textbooks written by one of the teachers, Elias N. Eliascos, a graduate of the school who went on to get a doctorate in linguistics. From one-third to one-half of the graduating class goes to university abroad, mostly but not exclusively to the United States. Fees are $600 for the 1,000 day students, $1,500 for the 250 boarders; but scholarships are available to all who can demonstrate inability to pay. A sister institution, Pierce College, is even more completely Greek in its program — only biology and home economics are taught in English — but received major assistance from the Agency for International Development for the construction of a three-million-dollar plant in the hills above Athens.

Among the most significant differences between the American schools and the French lycées with large numbers of local students is that on the whole the Americans have been less successful than the French in establishing their own language as the basic language of instruction. If all goes well, however, the John F. Kennedy School in Berlin will be able to function as an analogue to the Französischer Gymnasium of the same city. Except for German itself, all subjects in the secondary school will be taught in English or (in the case of the foreign languages) with English as the language of control. Even Latin, which is to be compulsory for the German but not for the other students, will be taught with reference to English. Most of the teachers will be English-speaking Germans, with a few key people imported from the United States. There will be no fees whatever; basic costs will be met by the city of Berlin, with a small contribution by the U. S. State Department. In 1965, with the first seven grades functioning in a former German Air Force laboratory toward the borders of the U. S. Zone, there was a waiting list of 2,000 German applicants. "We have twenty pre-natal registrations," said Rudolf Bewer, an American-trained (Springfield College) Berliner who is principal of the school. "Berlin parents are highly interested in bilingualism. And we offer a kindergarten program, an all-day school, bus service. The school is fashionable. And we carry a great name."

The school operates under a separate law, with a separate inspectorate from the Berlin government. There are two chairmen of the board — Professor Dietrich Goldschmidt, a sociologist working for a German foundation incorporated in the Max Planck Institute; and the cultural affairs officer of the U. S. Information Service, whoever he may be at the time. "According to the law," said a representative of the Berlin Education Ministry ("Senator for Schools") who has been closely associated with the Kennedy project, "the standards must be at the same level as those at the Berlin public schools. And to go to university the German students will have to have an *Abitur*. You must understand that the *Abitur* is the only final examination we have." Bewer went further. "We expect," he said, "many third-country nationals in the eleventh through thirteenth grades. Most Americans here are young. So we will need an *international Abitur*."

6

One further model is possible: that of the first-rate American private school. "We are here," said the Reverend John C. Patterson of St. Stephen's School in Rome, "to set up a demonstration of what American education can be abroad. I grew up in Argentina as an expatriate American, went through it all myself in Buenos Aires." An Episcopal priest, Patterson had been headmaster of Kent School in Connecticut from 1949 to 1962. He brought with him to Rome the former assistant headmaster of Kent; the former chairman of the Kent mathematics department, Robert E. K. Rourke, who had also been executive director of the original College Board mathematics reform project and co-author of the statistics and probability text which was its first reform; Emory S. Basford, former head of the English department at Andover; the novelist and critic Edmund Fuller, who had been teaching at Kent; a Harvard-trained science teacher from Choate and a Harvard-trained classics teacher from Andover.

The school rented and reconditioned a seventy-room modern Baroque mansion, full of *trompe-l'oeil* effects in the style of Gaudi, in the luxurious Parioli section of Rome; and the first classes were held in September 1964. Maximum enrollment, grades 9-12, is 150 students, of whom about 115 are boarders, living in hotels nearby, which St. Stephen's has rented for the academic year (leaving the owners free to take tourist business during the late spring and summer). Fees are $1,250 a year for day students, $3,000 for boarders.

All students must study either Latin or Greek and one modern foreign language, which need not be Italian (though those who take another modern language must also take a course in conversational Italian). Languages are taught by native speakers, most of whom have also had experience teaching in schools in the United States. The program is that of a modern New England boarding school, intellectually rigorous, with special attention to character-building, Christianity and athletics. The school has the use of the Olympic fields, gymnasia and pools, only a few minutes' walk from the villa.

Patterson, who is otherwise anything but parochial, likes to say that the school has students from twenty countries, which is more or less true: the parents are resident in twenty countries. But all the students are Americans, and the preparation is entirely for entrance to American colleges. Advanced Placement courses are offered in every subject. More than half the first graduating class, in 1966, was accepted at colleges where entrance is difficult — Amherst, Carleton, Colby, Duke, Harvard, Kenyon, Randolph-Macon, California (Berkeley), Pennsylvania and Wesleyan, among others. Apart from the financial problem, which is serious, the school is an obvious success — and, thanks to the hearty iconoclasm of Patterson and Rourke, a clear-headed and attractive place. It has greatly impressed Italian visitors, and seduced the children of U. S. Ambassador Reinhardt away from the Lycée Chateaubriand.

Its relevance to international education, however, is by no means clear. St. Stephen's has had enough struggles of its own, getting started, not to look for trouble in negotiations with European countries to win acceptance of the College Board Advanced Placement tests as an equivalent of domestic secondary examinations. Patterson and his staff are perfectly willing, even eager, to experiment with academic program, but not for the purpose of selling European ministries of education. Rourke, who is Canadian, would like to see the school try non-American students, and attended the first mathematics meeting of the International Schools Examination Syndicate to see whether the program being developed for the international schools was suitable for St. Stephen's. To the extent that the prospects for an international examination depend on the quality of staff to teach the program and students to write the papers, St. Stephen's would have much to contribute. In any event, it is good for the image of American schools abroad that Europeans should know something about this small but sparkling facet of the American system.

PART THREE

THE INTERNATIONAL EXAMINATION

CHAPTER 8: **The Prospects for a Passport**

In the best of all possible worlds there would be no examination for entrance to higher education. The people who run secondary schools, who have watched the growing adolescent work for some time, would be sufficiently capable, knowledgeable and sensitive to tell the people who run universities which of their graduates were and which were not good prospects for university work. Indeed, experience in the United States, where admitting authorities see both the child's grades at school and his external examination scores, indicates that the quality of past work in school is a far better prediction of ultimate success at university — almost but not quite regardless of the school — than any set of numbers from an examination. Suitably regressed, however, the examination scores improve the prediction possible from grade-point averages.

At the universities, those members of the faculties who have thought about these problems (not many of them have) care much more for the quality of the student than for the quality of his preparation. Most professors, in fact, regard even the finest secondary preparation as quite inadequate, requiring the universities to teach material which every entrant should already have mastered. And yet there is at every university a floor below which the student's performance may not fall: he must be able to execute the mathematics, read the language, write the papers, interpret the symbols. Jean Johannot, director of the Swiss school Le Rosey, speaking from far greater experience than anyone at a university, can say that "In mathematics there isn't much difference between what the American boy and the French boy *knows*. The French boy can *do* more, but he doesn't *know* more." At the university, nobody cares: the university program must necessarily be based on what the student can do.

"I keep saying to the West African Examinations Council," said George Bruce, head of the University of London examining board, thinking of many meetings where English and African educators have tried to hammer out the practicalities of specifically African secondary courses, " 'If you want the recognition of British universities, don't do *that*. If you don't care about the British universities, then go ahead.' "

Socially, the purpose of the university entrance examination is to adjust the number of successful applicants to the number of places. Pedagogically, the purpose of the examination is to assure the university that a student can perform those tasks which are considered essential for the work ahead. Where the society is prepared to restrict university entrance to the tiny fraction of the most obviously able — as it is in Denmark and to a slightly lesser degree in the Netherlands and Germany — the school can make the necessary determinations with a minimum of outside help. Where nearly everyone is to have some sort of chance at higher education, as in some of the United States, the school diploma can be accepted without embar-

The Prospects for a Passport

rassment on either side. But if a substantial yet limited fraction is to move up the educational ladder — to the more ambitious colleges in the United States, to the expanding but still inadequate universities of France and Japan — the problem becomes too difficult for the political, psychological and technical equipment of the schools. Neutral standards must be found and must be enforced by some kind of examination.

For the international school, the key question is the degree to which these neutral standards are in fact different from one country to another. If entering students at the universities must be able to perform very different tasks in the different countries, then no international school can hope to offer adequate preparation to a multinational group. But if the real standards are much the same — if they merely look different because of different cultural frostings on the cake — then some compromise program, to be taught in several languages, should be feasible.

On the surface, it would seem that standards must be very different from national system to national system. In Britain, the student comes to university from a two-year (even three-year) Sixth Form where he studied no more than three subjects, presumably to a considerable depth. In Germany, the student in the last year of *Gymnasium* in most states takes nine subjects. The average German student taking the *Abitur* is over 20; the average French student taking the *baccalauréat* is under 19. In the United States, the average high school graduate is not yet 18, and in Scotland the average entrant to university is not yet 18.

Very different proportions of an age group complete secondary education and advance to university in different countries, though it must be said that convincing statistics are hard to find. A recent study by the International Project for the Evaluation of Educational Achivement (I.E.A.) proclaimed that the percentage of the relevant age group in the "pre-university" year of secondary school in 1964 ranged from 70% in the United States, 57% in Japan and 23% in Sweden and Australia to 12% in England and Germany, 11% in France and 8% in the Netherlands.[1] But these figures are suspect — the American estimate is high; it is clearly not true that the proportions en route to university are higher in England and Germany than in France; and a 1964 Swedish figure of 23% for a system where the average candidate on the *Studentexamen* is over 20 years of age cannot be squared with other estimates, in the same book, that only 17% of Swedish 19-year-olds and 11% of Swedish 20-year-olds are still in school,[2] or with the fact that only 14% of the age group took the examination in 1962.[3] Still, differences of roughly this order unquestionably exist.

William D. Halls of the Department of Education at Oxford, who has been studying the plans for secondary education in different countries under assignment from the Council of Europe, estimates that in 1970 Sweden will send 21% of an age group to university, France will send 16%, West Germany 7% and Britain 5–6%. Comparable figures for the United States are difficult to come by, partly because the official Office of Education estimates have been shown to be inflated whenever checked and partly because an increasing proportion of American higher education takes place in junior colleges, some of which are genuinely part of a university system, some of which are a fairly low-level extension of secondary education (as, indeed, are a number of the nation's four-year colleges).

---

[1] Torsten Husén et al., *International Study of Achievement in Mathematics*, John Wiley & Sons, New York, 1967, Vol. I, p. 237.
[2] *Ibid.*, p. 231.
[3] Bengt Petri, "Some Facts About Higher Education in Sweden," in *The Intellectual Face of Sweden*, ERGO International, 1965, p. 17.

But something close to Halls' estimate for Sweden — perhaps a few percentage points higher — would seem roughly right for the United States.

It is very difficult to believe that an examination which helps select out 20% to 25% of an age group for the United States and Sweden can maintain the neutral standard expected by British and German universities accustomed to an examination which helps select out 5% to 7% of an age group.

2

Examinations take different forms in different countries. In the United States and under the new dispensations in Sweden, in Chile and in Brazil, the examination at the end of secondary school is multiple-choice and machine-scored; elsewhere, apart from a few experiments in Britain and in South America, examinations are constructed-response (i.e., the student writes his own answer) and hand-graded. In the United States the examination is over in a day (half a day for those who take only the aptitude test); in France, students are in the examining rooms for three days; in Denmark and Germany the examinations stretch out for nearly a month. The American Scholastic Aptitude Test is in essence a vocabulary test in English and mathematics and an intelligence test; all the other examinations (except the Chilean, greatly influenced by the American College Board–sponsored *prueba de aptitud académica*) seek to measure achievement in subject areas, as does the second half of the College Boards. In the Romance language countries and in Britain and the United States, the school-leaving test has historically been completely external, set and graded by people from outside the student's school. (In the United States, of course, the test is not and has not been the full determinant; the student's grades in school are also considered by the admitting authorities.) In the Germanic countries and Belgium, though some questions are set by national or regional authorities, the test has always had a high component of questions set and answers graded by the student's own teachers.

The results of this difference in procedure are many and significant. Where the examination is external and anonymous, the percentage of failures (or, on the College Boards, of obviously low scores) can be high — even, in the United States and France, higher than fifty per cent. Where the examination is internal, just another confrontation of school and pupil with an outsider observing benignly, very few will be permitted to fail. Thus, in countries like Denmark and Germany, the school undertakes to weed out applicants before they are presented for the examination. Because the failure of a candidate implies a criticism of the school, the numbers presented are much reduced, serving the social policy which offers only a small number of places at university. Students and teachers brought up in one of these traditions will clearly find it difficult to adjust psychologically to the other.

But the pressure of numbers is making changes everywhere — most spectacularly in France. The old *baccalauréat* was in two parts, the first of which was taken after six years of secondary education. Its passage was required for entrance into the seventh year, the *classe terminale*, where students would take a more specialized program, with nine hours a week of philosophy, or a dozen of math-physics for *Mathématiques-Elémentaires*, or ten of biology and biochemistry (*Sciences-Expérimentales*). A second examination stressing (but not restricted to) the specialized subject would yield the *bac* itself. In general, failure rates were high on the first, more general part of the examination, considerably lower on the second part.

In 1965, the first part of the *baccalauréat* was suppressed completely and apparently forever by the Ministry of Education, probably (the welter of argument surrounding this decision gives no grounds for certainty) because the burden of reading and grading all those papers had become too great for the staffs of the lycées, whose June and July were made horrible by huge bundles of paper. In the absence of the examinations, the *proviseurs* of the lycées were told to select, in the German manner, those students they believed would have passed the first part of the *bac* had it been offered. As the second part would still be anonymous and a French *proviseur* (despite the national direction of the system) needs all the friends he has in his locality, most *proviseurs* were fairly charitable in deciding whom to let through and whom to hold back. "We are indulgent," said Augustin Gaudin, former *proviseur* of the London lycée. "We know that this child lost his father, that child had whooping cough." But the result was greater-than-anticipated failure rates on the new one-part *baccalauréat*, with consequent uproar in the schools, the Chamber of Deputies and the press.

A second reform in the *bac* system, introduced simultaneously, greatly reduced the number of subjects on which the student would be examined in writing — again, obviously, to reduce the work load on the staff that would have to mark the papers (especially in the classics sections, where the same teacher handles French, Latin and Greek). To make sure that advance knowledge of the subjects to be on the written examination did not degrade the classroom work in other subjects (which were to be examined only orally, by the candidates' own teachers), the Ministry had question papers prepared for all subjects, and chose the actual examinations only a few days before their administration. The new system, incidentally, produced a *baccalauréat* without questions on French language and literature (which is not taught in the *classe termi-*

nale), infuriating the professors at the universities (who feel about their students' command of French much as their American counterparts feel about *their* students' command of English). In the future, one understands, all *bacs* will contain questions on French.

As the French moved part way toward the German system under the pressure of numbers, the Swedes began what will be a long trek toward the American system. All students in the last year of *Gymnasium* will be given objective standardized tests not unlike those of the College Boards, to be scored by machine. A national cut-off point on the test will be established to provide precisely the right number of entrants to universities, and each school will be told how many of its graduating seniors, comparing this school's results against national standards, are entitled to admission to university. The standard test score for each student will be sent to the school, but only as evidence for the school to use in determining (on the basis of the student's past school performance as well as his test score) who shall get the brass ring and go to university and have for life the right to wear the student's cap on May Day.

3

It all comes back, inevitably, to the question of level of achievement: what do each nation's universities expect their entering students to be able to do? What are the differences in real achievement in the secondary systems of the different countries?

This question is not answerable at any level of confidence whatever; the most we have are hints, some of them surprising. The reasons for the difficulty of the question are worth a few minutes' exploration.

By reading textbooks and visiting classes, it *is* possible to acquire some notion of what is being taught. But the relationship between what is taught and what is learned seems to be intensely complex, certainly not a linear function. Children unquestionably learn a great deal they are not "taught" — some of it true, some of it false — and they obviously do not learn a great deal that they are taught. "Forgetting curves" vary not only from person to person but also from item to item of material, so that even an accurate measure of what was learned today may be of little value in three months — and all systems give students at least three months between the end of secondary education and the start of university.

Even the examinations themselves are little help, because the grading patterns differ from place to place and because the relationship between the question and the course preceding its administration is obscure. It is one thing to ask a student to discuss the function of Edmund's soliloquy in *King Lear* if the class has studied a dozen Shakespeare plays; something else if four months have been given to the study of *King Lear*. The problem is particularly difficult in mathematics, because anybody can learn what look like advanced formulas if his teacher knows that only these formulas will be on the examination. Students at the Scholae Europaeae who wish to move on only to faculties in the humanities must nevertheless take two hours a week of mathematics through their final years, and must pass a mathematics examination on the European Baccalaureate. They are asked questions in the integral calculus, a fact which is on its face incredible. But year after year very similar problems in integral calculus are placed on the examination, and the visitor to the classroom finds the students dully grinding away on the handful of formulas which will suffice for just these questions. Honor is satisfied at the ministries, only two hours a week of class time are wasted, and the world is impressed, but it is sheer nonsense to say that these non-mathematical students have learned anything about integration.

Nobody can estimate what level of achievement is expected of students by reading examination questions without knowing what will be accepted as an answer and how stiffly the papers are graded. Traditionally, the French grade on a basis of 20 points; and until 1965 the passing grade on the *baccalauréat* (which was a pass-or-fail examination) was 9 — in American terms, 45%. Nor was a grade of 9 required in each subject: what was needed was an average of 9 for all subjects together. An absolute zero in any subject would disqualify a candidate, but he could pass with a 1 which was made up in some other area. Because each subject carried its own "coefficient," a good grade in, say, philosophy for an "arts" student could carry poor grades in, say, history, geography and physics. The *Philo* grade would be tripled in the final averaging, while the grades in history, geography and physics would enter the computation naked. With a 12 in *Philo* and a 2 in each of the others, the student would show a score of 42 for the four subjects, an average of 10.5, which was easily passing. Thus the great variety of subjects in which the French candidate was examined was deceptive — fairly concentrated study of a few specialties could produce the necessary results. Asked about a subject — *Sciences-Expérimentales*, for example, in the *Philo* option — a French lycée student in his last year would often reply, "We don't do much work for that: it has a low coefficient."

In the new *bac*, much of this technical detail has changed. As there are fewer subjects on the written examination — and what will be there cannot be predicted — each counts more heavily every day in school. Moreover, the simple pass-fail distinction is being abandoned in exchange for several degrees of passing. Ultimately, an average of 12 is likely to be required for entrance to university, with a score between 9 and 12 to offer access to jobs which require a *baccalauréat* and to lesser institutions of higher education, but not to university. The Office du Baccalauréat would also like to introduce a lower, third-level passing grade which would not entitle its possessor to a government job requiring a *bac* or to any further free education whatever, but would assure Machines Bull and Citroën and Air France that this particular job applicant had not completely wasted his time in secondary education. This tripartite pass level makes more difficult the construction of an international examination, because grades below the level necessary for university entrance on such an examination are not likely to be recognized officially or by private employers: for the French families at international schools, the risks of abandoning the *bac* are multiplied.[1]

In the German system, most of the states grade their secondary examinations to a base of 7, with an average of 4 (in American terms, 57%) required for acquisition of an *Abitur*. A grade below 3 in any one significant subject is usually enough to disqualify the candidate, so the examination is truly comprehensive, allowing for relatively little specialization. But here the "neutral" standards are absolutely unknowable, because much of the examination is oral and internal, with all the freak good luck and bad luck that can turn on which questions enters the examiner's head.

It is difficult to believe that differences of this magnitude in examination procedures are not reflected in students' future performance at university.

---

[1] This quick discussion gives no more than a hint of the extent or significance of the reforms in French secondary education and the *baccalauréat*. Describing the changes in the second cycle as they were announced in 1965, W. D. Halls wrote, "They represent the completion of what was begun in 1959 after DeGaulle acceded to power. In the space of a decade, by 1968 the face of French education will have been transformed out of all recognition." (*Schools, Society and Progress in France*, Pergamon Press, Oxford, 1965, p. 189.)

4

This observer's impression is that the Danish and German examinations rank highest in the educational *Almanach de Gotha*, with the British, French, Belgian and Dutch close behind, the nations of Southern Europe and the Eastern bloc sitting below the salt. Nevertheless, the Council of Europe treaty is a reality. Though the logic of the treaty is political rather than educational, and barriers to slow the interchange of students are high and effective, some motion does occur and the universities are not complaining of great differences in levels of preparation. Only the Greeks and the Turks seem to be seriously below the standards elsewhere, and in both cases the comparisons may be unfair: the Greeks must put an inordinate amount of time into studying different kinds of Greek, none of which is valuable to them when they travel; and the Turkish attitude in education is so completely directed toward accomplishment in science that even students from the French-, German- and English-speaking schools in Turkey seem to have language troubles when they move.

The Latin American and native Asian and African diplomas (saving only the Lebanese *bac* and the still colonial G.C.E.s awarded by parts of formerly British Africa) are given for much less performance. "The level is lower here and one must remember it," said the *proviseur* of the French lycée in Santiago de Chile. "One cannot live *in vitro*." American high school graduation is clearly several cuts below the minimum required at European universities. Traditionally, the Europeans (except for the English, who demand a Bachelor of Arts degree) have accepted American candidates only after the completion of two years of college work at home; while American colleges have accepted into their third year candidates who come with a European secondary certificate. Recently this pattern has been changing, and the better American colleges will grant only one year's advance in standing to the possessor of a European secondary diploma. In the best American high schools, moreover, about 50,000 students a year (more than two per cent of the graduating class, or something more than the entire group of *Abitur* candidates in West Germany) are taking Advanced Placement courses which appear to require only marginally less effort and accomplishment than the last-year courses in the European secondary schools. Students with three passes in Advanced Placement courses (passes are usually defined as grades of 3 or better on a scale of 5) are normally granted "advanced standing" — instant admission to second year. Recently as much as a third of the entering class at colleges like Harvard and Yale has been entitled to such preference (not all of them accept the offer).

Among the institutions which have declared an interest in an international university entrance examination are the American College of Paris and the American University of Beirut, which have suggested that they could offer a program leading to this examination for the benefit of students wishing to switch over to European universities. At present, the diplomas awarded at these institutions offer access only to careers in the Western Hemisphere. According to A. D. C. Peterson, head of the Department of Education at Oxford and director of the International Baccalaureate Office, these colleges believe they could complete an international baccalaureate program in their first year, and could offer a fair fraction of their freshman class for an international examination with reasonable expectations of success.

On this evidence, one can argue that in terms of general culture, it should be possible to construct an examination which would reflect the neutral standards of the European certificates and American Advanced Placement, probably requiring from most but not all American candidates a thirteenth year of schooling, to be recovered by entry to college as a sophomore rather than as a freshman.

5

But we are not dealing with questions of the level of general culture. In virtually all universities outside the Americas, and in many South American countries, a student is expected to specialize from the moment of entrance — indeed, admission is usually to a faculty rather than to the institution as a whole. Even in the United States, the best technical institutes will demand specialized preparation — Massachusetts Institute of Technology requires candidates to take the College Board achievement tests in mathematics and two of the sciences, and when consulted about the possible application of candidates who had passed an international examination the M.I.T. admissions officers said they would have to read the questions and probably the students' papers before they would be willing to abandon the College Board standard. In Britain, where admission is to a college within a university rather than to a faculty, the subject the candidate will "read" must be specified in advance — and students who feel they *must* go to Cambridge are well-advised to declare that they wish to read agriculture.

Expectations in Europe and at the best American science institutes, then, are not of some level of general achievement, but of achievement in specific areas. Thus, quite apart from the question of the level at which the subject is taught, the placement of topics on the secondary-school timetable may influence what students can do when they come to universities, and this placement varies drastically from place to place. In Germany, the study of physics begins at age 12 and continues, a few hours a week, through to the end of secondary education. In France, physics does not appear in the program until the beginning of the second cycle in the lycée, usually at age 15–16 (all previous science study was biological). Certain topics which are relatively fresh in the mind of the French student were covered millennia ago for the German student. Biology in the United States is taught in tenth grade, at age 15–16, and then vanishes for all but a handful of students.

The placement of topics by disciplines may be significant, too. There must be some residual effect from the fact that mechanics is studied as part of mathematics in Britain and as part of physics everywhere else. Even in subjects so closely linked together as mathematics and physics, it seems likely that universities in different countries have grown accustomed to students whose levels of achievement are higher in one or the other of the two disciplines.

Finally, pedagogical differences may have some effect, in terms of what the students can do. In Britain, in the new American courses and to a lesser degree in Germany, the teaching of science emphasizes experiments performed by the students; in France, in the old-fashioned American science courses and in Latin America, science is taught almost entirely by lectures and demonstrations. French mathematics courses (and science courses) demand from students at all ages great quantities of brute computation in problems where approximations and slide-rule estimates are acceptable elsewhere.

In recent years, comparative educationists have begun to attempt the measurement of what these differences mean, subject by subject, in terms of developed student capacity. It is an unbelievably difficult job even within a single country, where a known sequence of topics within the curriculum should enable a tester to assume, for example, that a student who passed an examination in differential calculus will be able to handle conic sections, polar coordinates and spherical trigonometry. When looked at seriously, such common-sense assumptions turn out to be false. A few years ago, in a study the results of which were never published, the Institut Pédagogique National in France examined accomplishment in four years' worth of mathematics by means of an examination given at the entrance to the second cycle of the lycée — at age 15–16. The scores by students, all of whom had passed the mathematics course of the preceding year, ranged from 2 to 18 out of 20, with perceptible numbers toward both extremes. Worse yet, teachers of mathematics at the end of the first cycle when asked about certain test items disagreed violently as to whether the items would be easy, reasonable or difficult for their students. On a number of items, the divisions of opinion on the staff were such that each of the three possible descriptions received about one-third of the vote.

In the United States, the quarrels about the validity of standardized tests, though annually put down by "scientific" reports from the Educational Testing Service, annually recur in more or less aggravated form. Unlike the European essay and constructed-response tests, the American tests are "reliable" — that is, a student will occupy about the same rank among his fellows on different forms of the test. But the accuracy of measuring something is not nearly so important as the significance of what is being measured.

In large part, the difficulty is one of specifying what the educational psychologists call "behavioral objectives" — which may range from an appreciation of democratic values or the ability to work in groups through a knowledge of where to look to find the boiling point of oxygen through an exact recall of the dates of the Roman Emperors. Discovery of the objectives that might be significant to future work (or life) is far beyond the capacity of either the educators or their research tools. It is occasionally a useful discipline for a teacher (or an admissions officer) to ask if a student can handle a certain question, and to learn that nobody knows whether he can or not. Even the verifiable statement that he gave this answer

The Prospects for a Passport

when asked this question in this way on this date may turn out to mean much less than it seems to mean, either positively or negatively. All the examinations — ritually in the case of the College Boards, covertly in the European countries — are the product of feedback from the rest of the educational system, and their validity can be no greater than that of the system they reflect.

To use such tools for cross-cultural comparisons of academic achievement is an act of breathtaking audacity, and the quality of the information produced cannot be very high. Still, it *is* information, many cuts above the ethnocentric guesswork which usually informs discussions of comparative academic standards.

6

By far the most elaborate study so far is that of the International Project for the Evaluation of Educational Achievement, in the framework of the UNESCO Institute for Education in Hamburg. The group's director is Torsten Husén of the University of Stockholm, and its ambitions include comparative studies in all disciplines. To date, the published material involves the measurements of 13-year-olds in 12 countries in reading comprehension, mathematics, science, geography and non-verbal ability (in a study now admitted to be not very good), and more elaborate measurements of mathematics only at age 13 and in the "pre-university year" of secondary education (in a study not yet admitted to be not very good). For students "specializing" in mathematics in the pre-university year, the more or less raw scores (corrected for guessing) showed a variation from a mean of 36.4 (out of 69) in Israel, 35.2 in England and 34.6 in Belgium to a mean of 13.8 in the United States, 21.6 in Australia and 25.5 in Scotland. For pre-university-year students not "specializing" in mathematics, the more or less raw scores showed a variation from a mean of 27.7 (out of 58) in Germany, 26.2 in France and 25.3 in Japan to 12.6 in Sweden and 8.3 in the United States.

Obviously, these scores are related to the age of the students in the pre-university group and to the proportion of the age group which is still in school (nobody not still in school was tested). Unless the selection devices within the school are arbitrary or worse, it must be true that the larger the group continuing in school, the lower the median score on any test given in the terminal year. The authors of the study have eliminated this factor from their comparisons — and thus determined the results of the comparisons — by the quite spectacular and clearly wrong assumption that the selection devices within the schools are *perfect*, that the 4% of a Belgian age group in the pre-university mathematics track is the exact equivalent of the *top* 4% of the American age group. The I.E.A. figures show 18% of the American age group in a pre-university mathematics track, so the top 22% of this sample (4:18=22:100) is taken for comparison against the complete set of Belgian scores. This calculation raises the United States median from 13.8 to 33.0, for comparison against the Belgian median of 34.6, and permits the authors to assert further that 3.2% of the total American age group reaches the 50th percentile of scores internationally on the test for mathematics students, as against only 2.8% of the total Belgian age group.[1]

But there is no reason to believe that all the Belgians no longer in school would in fact score below the international median on the I.E.A. test. At age 13, with everyone still in school, 45% of all Belgian scores fell in the range of the top

[1] All statistical correlations in the report are made further suspect by admitted mistakes in the calculations for Finland. See Alexander W. Astin, "Learning Mathematics: A Survey of 12 Countries" (Book Review), in *Science*, June 30, 1967, Vol. 156, pp. 1721–2.

22% of all American scores, and more than 70% of the Belgian children scored better than the international median, as against only about 40% of the Americans. No reasons are given why the readers (or the authors) of the study should assume a massive catching up by the Americans or falling back by the Belgians during the succeeding five years. Surely the authors cannot be so naïve as to believe that simply because adolescents leave school their education stops. And for university entrance purposes, of course, the only significant figures are those of the raw scores. Belgian universities can expect their average entrant from a secondary mathematics program to perform on whatever level may be implied by a 34.6 score on such a test, while American colleges can expect only the performance indicated by a 13.8 score.

Assuming the validity of the I.E.A. test itself (a large assumption), the comparative data are interesting from the standpoint of a possible international matriculation examination if certain other assumptions are made about the proportions which in fact succeed on the national examinations and are eligible for university. Let us assume for the United States the Conant estimate that 15% of an age group is preparing (or is capable of preparing) a genuinely academic program,[1] and assume further that this 15% is composed of one-half the students who are taking a mathematics course in their senior year and a little less than one-eighth the students in the senior year who are not taking a mathematics course. These samples can then be compared, also by assumption, with two-thirds of those in either program in the pre-university year in Europe.

If one then looks at the score made by the bottom member of each of these groups and takes it as a cut-off for university entrance, the result in the mathematics track is a score of 14 for

[1] James Bryant Conant, *The American High School Today*, McGraw-Hill, New York, 1959, p. 20.

the Americans, 22 for the Germans, 27 for the Belgians and French, and 28 for the English. Among students no longer studying mathematics (at all in the case of Americans and English, as a major subject in the other countries), the cut-off would be 21 for the Americans, 17 for the English, 20 for the Belgians, 22 for the French and 24 for the Germans. On these data, the American deficiency in mathematics for mathematics specialists would seem to be serious, probably greater than can be made up in an additional year. (Moreover, the American group tested ran only two months younger than the English and four months younger than the Belgian, though it was ten months younger than the French and fifteen months younger than the German.) In mathematics for general culture, however, the Americans going on to serious higher education do not on these assumptions seem disadvantaged by comparison with the Europeans — a particularly interesting point (if true) in the light of the fact that all the others, except the English, are still plodding through a compulsory mathematics program of some sort.

7

Among the deficiencies of the I.E.A. study is the fact that items on the test were drawn up and approved by "experts in mathematics education" rather than by mathematicians. Many of them are in effect mathematics vocabulary questions quite unsuitable for measuring what the universities might wish.[1]

[1] Though measurement for purposes of university entrance was not what I.E.A. sought to do, these two sentences are an attack upon the test and ought not to be printed without some illustration. The prize, perhaps, is item 3 on Test 7:
"What is the converse of the statement, 'If two angles are vertical, then they are equal?
  "A. If two angles are vertical, then they are not equal.
  "B. If two angles are equal, then they are vertical.

The Prospects for a Passport

More responsible to the disciplines, and thus more interesting, are the studies performed under the direction of William D. Halls of Oxford for the Council of Europe, involving only European educational systems. As of last report, comparative studies had been completed for this program in mathematics, physics and Latin.

Halls' studies illustrate many of the difficulties of constructing acceptable cross-cultural tests. In preparation for the con-

---

"C. If $\angle x$ and $\angle y$ are vertical angles, then $\angle x = \angle y$
"D. If two angles are not vertical, then they are not equal.
"E. If two angles are not equal, then they are not vertical."

The correct answer is B; but surely this question, asked of mathematics "specialists" only, deals with nothing at all but vocabulary.

Again, item 2 on Test 8 reads:
"If x and y are real numbers, for which x can you define y

$$y = \frac{x}{\sqrt{9-x^2}}$$

"A. All x except $x = 3$
"B. All x except $x = 3$ and $x = -3$
"C. $x < -3$ and $x > 3$
"D. $-3 < x < 3$
"E. $x < 3$"

The answer D merely verifies through a lot of folderol that the respondent (a mathematics specialist) has not been so confused by the question that he has forgotten that the square root of a negative number is not included in the set of "real" numbers.

There are others of like nature on the tests, most of them too complicated to criticize in a footnote. The best item of all, however, occurs in the test for 13-year-olds. It is item 12 of Test A, and it was inserted, we are told, to measure the effect of introducing "modern" topics:

"If $\frac{x}{2} < 7$, then

"A. $x < \frac{7}{2}$
"B. $x < 5$
"C. $x < 14$
"D. $x > 5$
"E. $x > 14$"

Only C is a right answer on the test, though A and B are in fact not necessarily wrong. But the student is asked to treat the inequality sign as the exact equivalent of an equal sign for the purposes of this item of "modern topics." What proponent of such topics would grant the validity of such an item?

ference to plan the physics test, British examiners on loan from the Oxford and Cambridge Schools Examination Board went over the questions asked on recent examinations in the thirteen participating countries and culled one hundred test items to be proposed for the international study. Not one of the hundred items was acceptable to the representatives of all thirteen nations; and fewer than a dozen were acceptable to a bare majority of the authorities represented at the meeting.

Where I.E.A. could say blithely that "There appears at the present to be a certain agreement internationally upon aims and contents and methods" in mathematics,[1] Halls had to live with the fact that the inspectors of mathematics in the different countries disagreed violently on questions of both content and pedagogy. I.E.A. managed the disagreements in part by stressing symbolic vocabulary (on which, indeed, a fair amount of agreement exists) and in part by proclaiming an "inclusive" test on which all nations would be to a degree punished by what they left out, a relatively acceptable proposition because each nation did leave out (or had taught years before) some of the topics tested. Halls and his staff had to negotiate compromises, as though they were building an examination for use in determining the future of real live students.

Halls' results are not quite so quantifiable as those of the I.E.A. project, but they indicate that no really major differences exist among the levels of achievement in mathematics and physics in the European countries. The Germans are far more proficient than anyone else in Latin, but the rest of the pack is bunched here, too.

[1] Husén et al., *International Study of Achievement in Mathematics*, Vol. I, p. 33.

The Prospects for a Passport

It should be kept in mind — as a fact, not as a criticism — that people are led by their opinions to the kinds of educational research they do. Halls is angry and contemptuous about the heavy concentration on two or three subjects during the Sixth Form years in Britain, and anxious to prove that a less specialized program does not lower levels of accomplishment. Husén and his colleagues are advocates of comprehensive schools and a minimum of selectivity, plus "progressive" methods of instruction. (They are thus, incidentally, delighted with the very strong performance of the Japanese on their tests from the point of view of comprehensiveness and the maintenance of large populations through secondary school, less pleased with possible implications that the authoritarian and memory-based Japanese methods of instruction are especially efficient.) The extent to which the studies reported are unconsciously biased by their proprietors' views is quite impossible to determine.

8

The ideal international university entrance examination has been proposed by T. Nelson Postlethwaite of the I.E.A. project (he wishes to share credit for it with D. A. Pidgeon of the National Foundation for Educational Research in England and Wales). On this plan, each school would draw up a "blueprint" of its "objectives and content areas," which would be "arranged in a two-way table . . . so that the separate cells in the body of the table may contain suggestions for specific questions or items." This blueprint would then be passed to a central organization which would have an enormous "item bank" out of which test items could be fed to form an examination hand-crafted to the specifications of each individual school. (A further check on the hand-crafting could be provided by giving the school itself a choice of several items from each cell.) "The examination," Postlethwaite writes, "is then exactly the one the school requires, since it has been prepared to fit the school's blueprint, the only difference being that the items have been prepared by experts (item-writing being a highly skilled task)."

For national school systems, each item in the bank would have been pre-tested on large sample populations to give norms and relationships between scores on the one item and anticipated scores on an entire test. The "passing" grade would be high in schools with unambitious programs and low in schools with ambitious programs. Postlethwaite postulates that for an international examination differences between national systems could be treated as equivalent to differences between schools in national systems. By keeping the item bank current for all countries, researchers could describe the "characteristics" of each item anywhere in the world.

"Since the characteristics of the item are known," Postlethwaite writes, "it is possible for the central organization to determine the characteristics of the examination as a whole. Furthermore, from previous evidence the central organization would know the cut-off point for either a 'pass' or 'entry to university' on the test in various countries. Thus grades or marks could be awarded in various national currencies to any student although the examination would be entirely school based. . . . About two or three preparatory years would be needed to assemble items with accurate statistics, establish norms, and to set up the necessary machinery for giving quick service both in supplying items for blueprints and scoring the results quickly. A trial run would obviously be necessary."

The Prospects for a Passport

Postlethwaite admits that "Such a scheme is not without problems which would need to be investigated by research." He lists four:

> 1. Stating the objectives of teaching (and hence the objectives of evaluation) in operational terms and producing examination blueprints are not easy and teachers would clearly require advice and guidance. . . .
> 2. Different schools may produce quite different blueprints, i.e., they may seek to achieve quite different objectives in their teaching (and hence examining) of the same subject. This might produce problems when it comes to writing appropriate items. . . .
> 3. If a school has one or more unique objectives, difficulties may arise in finding schools in which to try out items prepared to measure them. . . .
> 4. There is a psychometric problem involved in producing the different "national" characteristics of an examination from the known statistics of the items constituting it.

The only one of these difficulties to which Postlethwaite proposes a solution is the second (or perhaps the third: the difference between the second and third is a little obscure), where he is prepared to accept the need for a suggested syllabus in international schools. But the disagreements between the parties who try to plan international examinations (for I.E.A., for Oxford or for international schools) are not about the test items themselves but about the syllabi they reflect. In fact, the "objectives" of secondary-school teaching to candidates for university are in our imperfect world nothing more or less than the entrance requirements of the universities. These being unknown, and in some sense unknowable, no project along the lines of Postlethwaite's can be made practicable.

Nevertheless, the Postlethwaite paper, circulated at a conference on the international examinations problem in Paris in 1967, makes a considerable contribution. The procedures he suggests are ideal, and they form a reference standard by which to measure the examinations ultimately proposed for adoption.

9

More important than all the theories, of course, is the existence theorem — the fact that at all the Scholae Europaeae there is a functioning international examination. The written European Baccalaureate examinations comprise six subjects for each candidate. In the future the candidate will choose one of four options, including an examination with concentration in social sciences. In the past, there have been three options — classical languages, science and modern languages.

All candidates for the European Baccalaureate, whatever their option, take a four-hour examination in their native language, carrying a coefficient of 2.5 (i.e., for purposes of determining the total score on the exam, the score on this part will be multiplied by 2.5). Those in the classics section must also perform translations from Latin and Greek to their native language (three hours for Latin, three and a half for Greek; coefficients of 2.5 and 2, respectively); write a composition in philosophy on one of three suggested topics (three and a half hours, coefficient of 2); solve five required problems in mathematics (three hours, coefficient of 1.5), and either translate a passage from a modern foreign language into their native language or write a composition in the modern language (all four of the European Economic Community's languages plus English are offered for examination; three hours, coefficient of 1.5).

In the scientific section, there is a four-hour mathematics

test with five more difficult required problems (coefficient of 2.5); a translation from Latin to the student's native language (three hours, coefficient of 2); a two-hour physics test (two situations, with three to six questions on each; coefficient of 2); a philosophy composition and the same modern foreign language test given in the classical section (three hours and a coefficient of 1.5 for each).

In the modern language section, Latin is dropped, the first modern foreign language carries a coefficient of 2, and a composition in a second modern foreign language (description and discussion of a given text in the language of the text) is allotted three hours of time and a coefficient of 1.5.

The European examinations have been printed only for the years 1959 to 1962, as document 9279/63 of the Services de Publications des Communautés Européenes. They are in truth international examinations — the same problems are set in mathematics and physics, and the same passages for translation or discussion are set in ancient and modern languages, for students from all the six countries. Only in philosophy are the problems different, and even here the major difference is that by using a quotation from Kant or Schiller, Kierkegaard or Jaspers the German examiner gives the student a historical handle to use in gripping the problem, while the students from the other countries must start from scratch.

From an American point of view, the examinations of the European Baccalaureate are strange indeed. The three-hour translation from Latin involves a passage of no more than two hundred and fifty words, and the mathematics and physics problems would seem to be no more than an hour's work for a reasonably qualified student. In philosophy the students are asked to answer questions like "Is history a science?" and "Do you think it is a good idea to study philosophy in secondary school?" (On one of the Italian papers, the question was the stark "Merit or luck?") For some reason, different topics in philosophy are set for the classics section as against the others, though "What is the difference between a moral law and a scientific law?" turned up on both varieties of French paper in different years. To write for three hours on such a question without disgusting a grown-up examiner is surely one of the more difficult assignments that can be handed to a teen-ager.

In modern foreign languages, the European Baccalaureate seems to ask considerable mastery of formal style. In 1961, for example, the passage in English was the following extract from Ivor Brown's *Shakespeare*:

> I am not saying that the Elizabethan theatre, so young of growth, provided exact parallels to our distracted theatre, bedevilled as this is with film contracts, vast salaries, and the din and blaze of publicity. No doubt they took things more easily then, fussed less over "flops" and were less jumpy, prickly and vain. But, even so, there must have been emotional crises, rows and recriminations. Amid all that Shakespeare was writing his texts: madhouse and miracle went together.
>
> But he was the common-senseman always. He knew that miacles are only half miraculous; they come by taking thought and plodding on as well as by hit-or-miss methods and by the sheer luck of a moment's inspiration. He had a will of his own. "Would not be debauched." He had grown up among the dissolute bully-boys of the old brigade, of which Green was richly typical, down at heels and up in arms, cursing and quarrelling, drinking and drabbing, churning out a sufficiency of theatre-stuff to buy a stoup of liquor, and then rotting away in debt and disease. Shakespeare was fastidious; he had a nose and the filth of poverty offended him. He was going to rise clear above the squalor of Green's death. There was always behind him, too, the sweeter smell of the countryside, for which he craved not merely as a posy-loving poet but as a man of farming stock, a devotee of ownership and possession. With the actor's and the playwright's thirst for glory he mingled the

The Prospects for a Passport

land-hunger of a peasant. He had a wife and three children to keep, a family to restore, and hard work would do it. He had a home and acres in his mind's eye and very soon they were in his hand as well.

Loving beauty, from the eye of the wren to the starry floor of heaven, he loved women and paid for it. His masculine affections were warmed, too, by his eye for elegance. He opened his heart freely. He suffered deeply in body and mind in the middle reach of his life and almost laid laughter aside. He had lost his son and found a dark mistress who turned out to be a daughter of "the sugar'd game." He was more libertarian than libertine; for libertines fall behind with their work, and he was ever punctual with a new play, even while studying a new part to act for no good reason save his delight in the mumming of it and in roaring out the "eloquent rapsodooce." Libertines get into debts and he would rather a lender than a borrower be. His genius, as we see it now, far outranged contemporary awareness of it and it seems to have outdistanced his own notion of it too; there is no sign that he felt underrated as an author.

Students are given the option of translating this passage into their own language or answering in English the following three questions:

1. Why does Ivor Brown say that our modern theatre is: distracted, bedevilled with film contracts?
2. Do you think that theatre or film actors can easily live and have as normal a life as common citizens?
3. You have probably attended performances of Shakespearean plays. Can you tell us what you like or dislike in them?

What the outsider is to make of all this — what anybody is to make of it — is hard to say. The Latin and Greek translations and the mathematics and physics tests must be marked very severely; the translation from Brown's *Shakespeare* must be marked rather loosely; and nobody not trained in European pedagogy can begin to guess how the answers to the philosophy questions can be marked at all. The notion of cross-cultural marking of many of these papers is in itself a fine work of man's imagination.

One possible explanation is that the examination is not international at all, despite the identical questions in different languages. In the marking process the student may be thrown in competition not with the graduating class as a whole but only with others in his own linguistic group. Such a procedure would be sensible in the circumstances of the European Baccalaureate (the student, after all, seeks admission to his own national universities and not to some international university). Assuming that the Halls data on German superiority in Latin are correct, it would be relatively easy for the examiners to apply higher criteria to translations from Latin into German than they would apply to translations from Latin into other languages — indeed, the variation would occur automatically.

Yet teachers at the schools do seem to feel that the students from the different groups are being compared against each other. In mathematics, in physics and in the second foreign language for the "modern" section (where the examination consists of a composition in the language being tested), such cross-cultural comparisons can certainly be made. Moreover, all the schools are in agreement that English is more difficult for the Italians than for the others, and the Italian group now starts its instruction in English a year earlier, in the second rather than the third year of secondary school.

Originally, the examinations were written by committees drawn from the national ministries; since 1966, the examiners have relied more on suggestions from teachers. The European

Baccalaureate is given in three parts, two of them internal to the school, and it is more than possible that in the final weighting the in-school examinations are counted heavily. The students themselves, however, take the external examination seriously enough that once when it was administered an hour earlier in Luxembourg than in Varese some boys kept a telephone line open between the two schools to pass on information from candidates in Luxembourg who felt an overpowering need to go to the bathroom right after reading the questions.

Still, crude as the instruments obviously are, they work. The European Baccalaureate has made it possible for the Scholae Europaeae to teach the same subjects on the same schedule to four different linguistic groups, and to pass them all on to their home universities officially certified as prepared for higher education. And there have been no complaints from the universities.

CHAPTER 9: **The International Baccalaureate Office**

The attempt to found an international university entrance examination for the benefit of students at private international schools can probably be traced to a speech by Albert van Houtte of the Scholae Europaeae at a meeting of the International Schools Association in 1957. Relatively few of the international schools had at that time reached the stage of preparing students for universities. Van Houtte's initiative was ignored, and the topic was forgotten.

Within five years, however, the question had become one of some urgency, and I.S.A. took up the matter with UNESCO, which eventually awarded a grant of $2,500 for preparation of a report on the possible organization of international school programs around a social studies "core." (Science would be taught historically, stressing the contributions of scientists of all nations, etc.) This being a rather bad idea at best — the head of a French multinational school says he would prefer not to teach history at all: "It's a lot of Gaullist nonsense" — the report was suitably buried with conventional rites of mimeographing as a UNESCO document.

Meanwhile, the history department of the International School of Geneva, under the leadership of its chairman Robert Leach (who had spent the academic year 1961–62 visiting international schools all over the Northern Hemisphere), had prepared a draft syllabus and examination for a course in "Contemporary History 1913–63," and four terminal students at Ecolint had sat the examination in June 1963. One of the four was admitted to Harvard, which accepted his international history course as the equivalent of an Advanced Placement credit. Copies of the syllabus and examination were distributed to ministries of education all over the world, and forty responses were received — "for the most part highly encouraging."[1]

Pleased by the reception of their maiden effort in what they considered "the most controversial field in international schools," the leaders of the English side of the Geneva school formed an International Schools Examination Syndicate (now International Baccalaureate Office), which was juridically attached to Ecolint pending formal organization as an independent body under Swiss law. The staff of the school, virtually unaided and without compensation, proceeded to put together "the outline of a curriculum for an International Baccalaureate," which was completed by the end of the school year in 1964.

Recognizing the transiency of international school students (and doubtless influenced by the Sixth Form model),

---

[1] Statement of Basic Principles of I.S.E.S.

the Geneva teachers designed a pattern of two-year courses leading to the examination. In history and world literature, the course outlines were more or less original; the other subjects were represented by outlines quite similar to a national program, usually British (the mathematics course was specified as that of the Southampton project), French in philosophy, American in biology. Although the policy statements of the group stressed the full internationalism of I.B.O. by contrast to the European parochialism of the Scholae Europaeae, the fact was that neither the world literature nor the philosophy outline ventured east or south of Tolstoy and Plato, and each contained only one author west of the Welsh marches. Leach's history examination, however, inspired by his own vast reading, wrestled with the problem of the "outer" world.

Although these first steps were taken pursuant to a request by the International Schools Association, in fact the base of the effort was extremely narrow: I.S.A. itself was fundamentally the creation of Ecolint. And the principles on which the work was performed were Anglo-American in the highest degree. "It has been the contention of the staff of the International School of Geneva," said the statement of these principles, "that the preliminary negotiations between and among national educational authorities would in fact result in a politically motivated stalemate. It is better to seek from individual universities an *exception* in favor of an individual candidate, on the basis of his performance on an individual examination (or group of examinations). The standard intentionally developed in the pilot examination is higher than that exacted by any one national examination system. The standard of the International Baccalaureate is intended to be that of the highest common denominator between and among the better national systems (both Occident and Orient). It is expected that *exceptions* in favour of individual candidates will in a few years become *rules* in favour of the International Baccalaureate. It is also expected that as the Baccalaureate becomes widely accepted its usefulness in providing a standard for the interchangeability of academic work throughout the world will prove invaluable."

Such procedures can work, of course, only in English-speaking universities, and not in all of those. In continental Europe, in Latin America, and in many parts of Asia and Africa, universities are forbidden by law to make exceptions for individuals. And what was under discussion at Ecolint was not, indeed, an international university entrance examination. It was, inevitably and not discreditably, a school-leaving certificate for the International School of Geneva, which would be recognized by universities, by other schools similarly situated, eventually by the whole world.

With the arrival of a grant from the Twentieth Century Fund, the base of the effort was widened — but not its focus. Fundamentally, the assumption was that the teachers at the specifically, international schools (overwhelmingly British in nationality) knew what they were doing, and that the other participants at the subject matter conferences would only suggest minor amendments to the proposals from the International School of Geneva or (occasionally) Atlantic College. People were invited not as bargainers for their own national systems, but as sympathizers with the Geneva project.

Intellectually and practically, value was most likely to come from meetings on the teaching of the different subjects if people who understood and valued their own systems were introduced to the values cherished in other systems and forced to wrestle with the disparities. There was a danger that a project for an international examination would draw to its meetings people who were unhappy with their national systems and who, rather than negotiating for their side, would welcome the new idea as a lever to be used for change at home. I.B.O. invited the danger. Participants in the meetings who raised objections based on national experience, like George Bruce of the University of London examining board or Robert E. K. Rourke of the College Board Commission on Mathematics, were considered hostile and were not invited back.

Parochialism created false perceptions of reality. "International education" was seen not as an undefined term represented institutionally by a number of struggling and confused schools, but as an established procedure intrinsically *better* than any national system of education. Gérard Renaud, assistant director of the International Baccalaureate Office, wrote in the autumn of 1967 in a guide for teachers at international schools that the I.B.O. "experiment is not impeded from the start by imperatives due to tradition, firmly anchored conceptions, etc., as can be the case in national systems. More exactly, the sole imperative is pedagogical efficacity. It would therefore be a grave error to attempt, on any pretext, a kind of compromise with traditional systems: if this were the aim, the project would lose all significance." Through the enterprise, a bright thread in the fabric, runs a search not for the acceptable but for the ideal, not for the informative but for the philosophically true, not for the useful but for the admirable. The story of Geneva's quest for an international examination thereby becomes rather touching, but sometimes inconsequent.

Building the European Baccalaureate, van Houtte and his colleagues first found the 70% overlap among existing curricula and examinations, then compromised the remaining 30%. Looking for an international examination, the Geneva group at no time analyzed — or even collected — the existing national examinations. In mathematics and physics, analyses of the national curricula and examinations, topic by topic, had been made by Oxford for the Council of Europe, and at one of the mathematics meetings a participant in fact had a copy of a draft of this study. But he did not place it on the table: despite Oxford's close connection with the International Baccalaureate project, he assumed that the material was confidential. At no I.B.O. meeting was any participant seen with so obvious and easily available a tool as the annually published book of questions and sample answers to last year's French *baccalauréat*.

The failure to produce staff papers outlining the apparent issues to be resolved left each conference on a subject area without a significant agenda. Much time was therefore occupied with the phenomenon John Maynard Keynes once described as the determination of how many votes Brazil should have on a commission where decisions would not be taken by voting. Nevertheless, the meetings were sometimes productive of important discussion, and even of decision.

2

Between the spring of 1965 and the end of 1967 there were about thirty meetings to work on aspects of the proposed international examination. All but two of them were meetings of "subject panels," usually composed of five to ten teachers with one or two representatives from universities in attendance. Ecolint and Atlantic College were represented at virtually all meetings, and half a dozen other schools at one or more of them. Nobody was paid for attendance at these meetings or relieved of other duties to prepare for them, and no meeting lasted longer than three days.

The first of the two large meetings was held in Geneva in 1965. Five subject panels — in history, geography, biology, languages and mathematics — worked separately for about half the time; a "technical committee" (labeled the *sixième bu-*

reau) and a pair of plenary sessions considered the larger problems of establishing an international examination. Academically, the problem areas were identified as mathematics, physics and languages. Though history and geography seemed sensitive subjects at first blush (and an expansion of the project to include students from Communist nations would doubtless produce difficulties in these subjects not encountered in exclusively non-Marxist groups of teachers and scholars), in fact representatives of different countries can usually agree with good grace on the need to present various national biases and to accept a variety of emphases. People are conscious of the ethnocentricity of their views of history and the social sciences. But few are prepared to admit that the differences between French and English views of mathematics may be as considerable and as legitimate as the differences between their views of history. The compromises which come easily when the subject under discussion is "controversial" are extremely difficult to achieve when the question is one of teaching mathematics or of measuring a student's understanding of a foreign language. Differences which are in truth national biases are perceived by even sophisticated people as questions of levels of accomplishment.

It is difficult to put a finger on the precise nature of these biases. In chemistry, different national programs place different degrees of emphasis on areas the physicists consider quantum mechanics. Britain and Denmark venture further into the calculus, France looks harder at topological problems. In physics, the French emphasize electrical phenomena and statics more than anyone else; the Germans have abandoned statics before examination time arrives. Perhaps the most easily visible gap is in the treatment of foreign languages, which caused perhaps the most extended argument of any in the subject panels. The British demanded passages to be translated from the language being examined to the language of instruction; the Germans would not accept any examination which included translation passages; the French were prepared to go either way on translations, but required a *thèse* (a composition in the language being examined, based on a one-sentence philosophical or literary question), which the English regarded as too difficult. Ultimately (at a third meeting), the British dropped their demand for translations, which would be clearly unfair when the language of instruction was the native language of some students but not of others.

Conflict persists in all these subjects. A third meeting of the physics panel closed the report of its deliberations with the comment that "much was still to be done before a full report in Physics should be produced for international circularisation." It should be noted, however, that the meeting in these subjects have seemed to observers by far the most interesting of the project. Differences in approach being too great to be papered over by sympathy for the goals of the project, the participants have worked harder.

The most serious technical difficulty to emerge at the first general meeting was a disagreement as to the degree of specialization desirable in the last years of secondary school. Speaking for the University of London, George Bruce doubted the acceptability of examinations which cut to any noticeable degree below the A-level standard. Speaking for the French Ministry of Education, E. van Smevoorde doubted the acceptability of any examination which permitted the student himself to select subjects individually. Each side, however, understood and to a degree sympathized with the objectives of the other. The schema adopted by the meeting — as a consensus, without a vote — required passes in seven subjects: one each from the language of instruction, the first foreign language, history/geography/philosophy/economics, and mathematics/science, plus three ad lib from a long list of possibilities. Three subjects would be required at a "higher" level and four at a "subsidiary" level for the full International Baccalaureate.

Later, on representations from virtually all the subject panels — which could not see how they could prepare the course they wished to teach as one of seven the students would have to take — the number of required examination subjects was reduced to six, and the foreign language was struck from the list of subjects that could not be omitted. (This change was dictated by the needs of students who wished to enter medical faculties, which would almost certainly demand Latin, mathematics, biology and chemistry of all candidates; such students would have to take seven examinations if the I.B.O. requirements also included the language of instruction, a social science *and* a modern foreign language.) The science panels broadened the language of instruction examination by successful insistence that technical and informational material, not only literature, be included in that examination. And a further change in the over-all pattern of the program was achieved by the philosophy panel, which successfully inserted a compulsory twice-a-week course in "Theory of Knowledge," which would not, however, be examined at the end. The course was a concession to the French taste, and would, like the French philosophy syllabus, include not only Platonic, Scholastic, Cartesian and Kantian speculation but also the speculations of the modern "scientific" psychologists.

One other issue raised and tentatively resolved at the first meeting has remained to plague all subsequent discussions: the amount of mathematics that should be required for the full certificate. It is a very old problem. Plato had inscribed over the gates to his Academy the words "Let none who has not learnt mathematics enter here." In the nineteenth century, the *pons asinorum* which braying candidates for Oxford and Cambridge had to cross consisted of an elementary Euclidean proof. Clearly, mathematics has grown increasingly necessary to study at university over the last two decades: a reasonable mathematical background is now essential for anyone who wishes to do serious work not only in physics and chemistry but also in biology, medicine, economics, sociology, psychology, linguistics or philosophy.

Nevertheless, the proposal that the full certificate should be awarded only to those who had passed an examination in mathematics, on higher or subsidiary level, was firmly resisted by the mathematics teachers, who had suffered enough through the unhappy experience of drilling unmathematical children to the monkey-work of "solving" the standardized problems of a pre-set examination. The mathematics teachers were supported by conferees who wished to leave students free to take courses and an examination in art or music. An unstable compromise, which has shakily survived all subsequent meetings, established a requirement of "mathematical literacy," which could be satisfied ideally by certification from within the school, if necessary by passage of a brief examination covering simple topics in intermediate algebra, theory of numbers, elementary plane and solid geometry, probability and statistics.

3

I.B.O. came out of the 1965 meeting a going concern with friends but no established organization. Its governing Council was chaired by John Goormaghtigh, Belgian in nationality, resident in Geneva as head of the European branch of the Carnegie Endowment for International Peace and also chairman of the board of Ecolint; the other members were G. Panchaud, Swiss, professor of education at the University of Lausanne; J. D. Cole-Baker, head of the English side at Ecolint; a scientist of Indian nationality from the International Telecommunications Union; and a former member of the administration of the elementary schools of the canton of Geneva. The executive committee which was to do the actual work was composed exclusively of teachers at Ecolint, to whose number a few teachers from Atlantic College were presently added. Its executive secretary was a teacher from Ecolint seconded to the project. Its first "examining board" was drawn entirely from the faculty of the Institut des Hautes Etudes Internationales in Geneva (which was reasonable, as the only subject then being examined was history). The chairman of the examining board was Jean Siotis, a Greek national who had completed his secondary education and taken his B.A. in the United States (University of Chicago), and secured his doctorate at the Sorbonne with a dissertation in French.

Of this group, only Panchaud and Siotis were *au courant* with the problems, and they were both more often at odds than at peace with the rest of the operation. From mid-1965 to mid-1966, I.B.O. staggered through a series of personnel crises, questionable financial allocations and unsatisfactory panel meetings, while the Council resisted any expansion of its membership which would diminish the influence of Geneva.

One significant addition to the Council was made, however, in 1965: A. D. C. Peterson, director of the Oxford University Department of Education, whose assistant W. D. Halls simultaneously became part of the working executive committee. In 1966, when negotiations for a larger grant from the Ford Foundation began to lag, Oxford moved reluctantly but firmly to take over the project. Peterson agreed to serve as director of I.B.O. part-time until January 1967 and full-time (on his sabbatical leave) for six months thereafter. Under his leadership, the internationalization of the I.B.O. Council was finally accomplished. The new members included Mme E. Hatinguais, *Inspectrice-Générale* and head of the experimental lycée at Sèvres, the *grande dame* of French education; Jean Capelle, *Recteur* of the University of Nancy and former chief of the permanent civil service of the Ministry of Education; and Harper Hanson, director of the Advanced Placement program of the College Entrance Examination Board, who was officially representing his employers. A former teacher of German at Williams College in Massachusetts, who had done his graduate work in Alsace, Hanson blended the academician and the test administrator in a peculiarly useful and intelligent way. Later additions to the Council include officers of Swedish, Ugandan, Moroccan and Lebanese universities, and of the Ministry of Education in Cameroon and in Poland.

The first fruit of the Ford grant of $300,000, to cover work over a three-year period, was a second large planning meeting, labeled the First International Baccalaureate Conference, held at Sèvres in February 1967, with an initial cocktail party at UNESCO headquarters in Paris as a kind of pat on the back. The conference lasted three days, and thanks to the professional Oxford management it proceeded on an established agenda backed by adequate working papers. Among the participants were representatives of British, Bulgarian, French, Swedish and Swiss universities; of the ministries of education in France, Poland, Tanzania, and two of the German states; of the Oxford and Cambridge Schools Examination Board, the College Entrance Examination Board and the French Office du Baccalauréat; of the British Council and the Ford Foundation. All meetings were devoted to procedural problems rather than substantive questions in the subject areas.

The proposal brought to the conference by Peterson was for experimental approval of the I.B.O. examination to be taken by no more than 500 students a year for six years. Oxford would supervise an extensive follow-through study to show how the graduates of international schools fared at university on the basis of I.B.O. preparation, and at the end of the six years there would be enough hard information to confirm the validity of the examination or to throw it in the dust heap. The first candidates would be offered strictly on the basis of an I.B.O. certificate in June 1970.

The meeting produced one major accomplishment: a compromise on an issue that had threatened to separate the United Nations International School from the project. Through its chemistry teacher John Gunnell, UNIS had proposed a sliding scale of marks with no pass/fail cut-off. Resident in America, UNIS had been able to get all its graduates into some sort of college on the basis of even low College Board scores (and to get its Europeans into Vienna or the Sorbonne as foreign students, a category for which these universities have, in effect, no entrance requirements). If I.B.O. awarded nothing whatever, the French delegation proved surprisingly receptive to a full certificate, UNIS would find it hard to abandon College Boards.

Peterson and Halls had rejected the idea of a sliding scale, because the continental Europeans would not be interested in anything but a pass/fail standard. At the conference, however, the French delegation proved surprisingly receptive to a scheme by which students who had not qualified for the I.B.O. certificate of university entrance could be given a separate certificate listing the subject examinations they had passed. Desmond Cole of UNIS agreed that this paper would probably be sufficient for many American colleges, and the crisis was over.

In general, however, the atmosphere of the conference was something less than confident. Discussions suffered from the transiency that bedevils everything having to do with international schools. Many of the delegates had not attended any previous I.B.O. meeting, and the working papers offered them assumed a background they did not have. Much territory that had been beaten over at previous conferences had to be explored again — especially at the final plenary session, which attracted a number of prominent people who had attended neither previous conferences nor previous sessions of this one. Because all the delegates were more or less volunteers, the conference attracted a mostly adventurous group, who found the syllabi and the scheme a little conservative and were blithely oblivious to the I.B.O. problem of shepherding the examination past the people in their ministries who were *not* dissatisfied with the existing national examination. A discouraging yet sometimes refreshing breath of reality was blown across the table occasionally by a retired official of the Swiss Federal Maturité, who asked intelligent questions, listened patiently (smoking his pipe) to the answers, and concluded each colloquy with the words, "That's very interesting, but it's not the way we do things in the Swiss Federal Maturité."

Bulgaria dramatically and officially accepted the I.B.O. certificate as sufficient credential for entrance to the University of Sofia, by a declaration at the conference itself. Peterson in the succeeding months persuaded 14 British universities to accept I.B.O. documentation as the equivalent of a continental certificate, won approval from the universities of Geneva, Zurich and Saint Gallen, and in a great triumph, in December 1967, secured recognition of the examination by the French Ministry of Education as a possible substitute for the *bac* for all applicants (including French applicants) actually resident outside of France. In the United States, where Peterson spent the summer of 1967 teaching at the University of California in Berkeley, the participation of Hanson gave good reason to believe that the colleges would consider the I.B.O. certificate as the equivalent of three passes at Advanced Placement.

In June 1967, experimental examinations were offered in

history and geography at Ecolint, in Latin and physics at Atlantic College, and in modern foreign languages at both schools. Outside examiners from Germany, Britain and Sweden participated, and on the whole professed themselves satisfied with the level of both questions and students. (The Swedish examiner's verdict that 14 out of 20 history candidates had reached *baccalauréat* or *Abitur* standards was a little chilling, however, considering the minor role of history in the French and German timetables for the last year and the major role of history at Ecolint.) By autumn, chief examiners had been appointed in ten subjects. Three of them were from Britain, two from France, two from Switzerland, one each from Germany, Sweden and the United States. The question of their function remained unsettled in the absence of an established examination-writing group — or, in the case of the most internationally distinguished of them, the economist John Vaizey of the University of London, the absence of even a tentative syllabus which could be the foundation of an examination.

His sabbatical having expired, Peterson returned to Oxford in September 1967, retaining on a part-time basis the overall direction of I.B.O. His full-time resident assistants were Gérard Renaud, who resigned from his teaching post at Ecolint to take the job, and Jack Sellars, an experienced educational administrator on two-year leave from the Inner London Education Authority. The target for the academic year 1967–68 was the preparation of examinations in all subjects, whether or not there were students ready to take them. For the academic year ending June 1969 it was hoped that the further $1.2 million needed to finance the six-year experiment would be in hand, and that, to begin with, students in at least three schools — Ecolint, UNIS and Atlantic College — would be taught on an I.B.O. syllabus.

4

The booklet on *The International Baccalaureate*, published by I.B.O. (then still known as I.S.E.S.) shortly after the Sèvres conference, stresses five research studies which would be carried on during the proposed six-year experiment:

> a. Assessment of the extent to which students with very varying preparation up to the age of sixteen could follow a curriculum of this sort for two years, and thus equip themselves for work in the specialised faculties of European Universities. This could be of great interest both to developing countries and to those European or American universities which receive large numbers of students from them. . . .
>
> b. Assessment of the relevance of concepts, skills and information acquired in the last two years of secondary school to those actually used in university courses. The fact that the I.S.E.S. research unit could compile, by the end of the experiment, between two and three thousand dossiers of students, who had entered universities in many different countries, would provide an unusual opportunity for this type of research.
>
> c. Assessment of the extent to which students who, in the last two years of secondary education, had followed a course deliberately designed to ensure a general education and to keep open the options between faculties at the university, could, in fact, meet the real requirements (not the entry "hurdles") of those faculties. This would be of particular interest in England where it is often assumed that this would be impossible. . . .
>
> d. Enquiry into the validity, reliability and "backwash" effects of different types of examinations — e.g., oral examining (as opposed to "interview"), objective testing, submission of "project" work, assessment of course work.
>
> e. Curriculum development. The design of the International Baccalaureate would be associated with a comparative

study of the content of education in the terminal classes of European and American secondary schools. The existing proposals have some claim to embody the best of national systems and also to have made some valuable innovations. To give them a trial would in itself be a useful contribution to curriculum development....

The list reveals both the strengths and the weaknesses of the International Baccalaureate effort. The questions posed are fascinating to intellectuals in education, and fully explain the addition of the resources of Oxford to the fumblings of the schools themselves in promoting the examination. But the topics proposed are too grandiose for the resources available, claim too much for the work already done, and reveal to those involved from near the beginning of the project a rather disheartening lack of self-education by its leaders during the developments of the last three years.

It has become apparent, for example, that the educational leadership of the developing countries is not in the least interested in a program which will make more efficient the selection of students to go off to American and European universities. On his tour of South America in the summer of 1967, Desmond Cole of UNIS was told at several ministries that while they might or might not find such an examination an acceptable substitute for foreign national examinations for those wishing to attend South American universities, they would not under any circumstances permit it to be used for the purpose of draining their nationals away. To some extent, the initial grants from the Twentieth Century Fund and the Ford Foundation were raised on the argument that an international syllabus and examination would be particularly useful to developing nations seeking to escape formerly colonial ties. Newcomers to the project still like this argument, which is, indeed, superficially convincing. But every exploration in this direction for three years has indicated that those educators in the developing nations who do wish for major changes in their secondary education resent the European rather than the colonial tie. To the extent that they must retain a European complexion in their secondary program, they are more than happy to continue with that of the former mother country, which without exception they consider the "best."

Again, experiment with "objective testing" has been part of the I.B.O. agenda almost from the beginning; but if the meeting at Sèvres produced consensus on any disputed item, it was that I.B.O. could not do much with objective testing. Introducing such tests in subject matter to Britain, the University of London spent almost $40,000 on part of an O-level chemistry test alone. The norming and ranking of items on these tests requires a stable student population large enough to permit the use of sampling techniques, neither of which conditions the international schools can meet. Moreover, College Board experiments in South America argue strongly that the translation of "objective" items from one language to another is very chancy, and strongly affects the reliability of the test. A European or Latin American ministry interested in trying out objective testing for its own purposes would be foolish to rely on I.B.O. as any kind of guide in this area. The use of such testing on the international examination at present must be an argument against its acceptance rather than an argument in its favor.

Most serious, however, is the I.B.O. "claim to embody the best of national systems." No comparative studies of the national syllabi have been made to give substance to such a claim. It is one thing to tell specialists in a country that a topic they teach in their secondary schools has been omitted from an international program because of the exigencies of time in an extraordinary situation, and something else to say it has been omitted because in somebody's judgment (somebody who may know little of the topic and nothing of the country where it is taught) this country's approach does not qualify among the "best" of national systems.

Finally, the third of the I.B.O. objectives exposes yet again the heavily English orientation of the project as a whole. The examination proposed is in fact rather more specialized than that of the European systems, yet research is to be directed particularly toward demonstrating that its non-specialized character prepares a student adequately for work in an English university.

Even in 1967, I.B.O. was still influenced by the quest for international purity which had reduced the membership of the International Schools Association during a time of vast expansion of multinational education. Nobody from the French overseas lycées or a member school of the International Schools Services was to be seen at Sèvres; and the supposed spokesman for the Scholae Europaeae was not someone who had ever run such a school or taught in one, but an *Inspecteur-Général* of the French ministry who had participated in some of the European Baccalaureate negotiations. Looking for more candidates than could be supplied by UNIS, Ecolint and Atlantic College for the first years of the International Baccalaureate examination, the governing Council of I.B.O. thought hopefully not of the French foreign lycées or the embattled American overseas schools but of Eton in England and Andover in America. Adjustment of the examination to the needs of binational schools — where the vast majority of the students who could be served by such an examination are to be found, and where the present expansion is most rapid — still lies in the future.

CONCLUSION

The International Baccalaureate Office may win acceptance for its examination on the terms so far requested. The money that would be required to support the institution of the examination and the associated research for six years is relatively minor as education budgets go — certainly less than two million dollars. For this introductory period, moreover, I.B.O. is talking of at most 500 and more likely 300 candidates a year, world-wide, of whom about 85% would receive the full certificate. Of those who succeeded on the examination, the great majority would surely be obvious university material by anyone's measure. In short, neither the governments nor the universities are being asked to risk anything of substance.

Unfortunately, what is being offered by I.B.O. to the participating schools will probably limit their number. The approvals granted by the British universities recognize the new examination as the equal of the French *baccalauréat*, which does not always mean the equal of the General Certificate of

Education. As the division of the London lycée demonstrates, a French *baccalauréat* is not perceived in England as a sufficient credential for English students. The French approval, while remarkable and encouraging, is from a parent's point of view rather ominously conditioned, for the Ministry has reserved the right to examine candidates' scholastic dossiers individually, and to reject I.B.O. certification if the dossier is not satisfactory. Thus neither the English nor the French group in international schools can easily abandon the G.C.E. and *bac* programs at this stage except in the few schools, like UNIS and Ecolint, where the parent body has political influence.

At the American universities, moreover, there is an increasing tendency to demand Scholastic Aptitude Test scores even from foreign candidates. On present plans I.B.O. will not seek exemption from these tests for American candidates; instead, the effort will be to secure recognition of the International Baccalaureate as the equivalent of Advanced Placement examinations. But actual admission is governed by Scholastic Aptitude Test scores; Advanced Placement scores are not in fact used for this purpose. (Colleges have already made and announced their admissions decisions before the Advanced Placement tests are administered; Advanced Placement scores are used solely to place a student in the right program after admission to college.) At the Educational Testing Service, indeed, the Advanced Placement procedure, with its partial reliance on essay questions rather than on standardized items, is regarded as technically indefensible: "The only way I can accept these tests," said Robert Valentine, the Educational Testing Service representative at the 1967 I.B.O. conference in Sèvres, "is on the argument that really they don't make much difference in the student's future." In any event, the assumption that Americans have no entrance problems is one which I.B.O. will have to sell the American contingents at the schools.

Conclusion

But what I.B.O. has done in less than three years may provide the groundwork for success in the future. Some difficult issues have in fact been resolved. The idea of separate examinations in six subjects, retaining the British and American election of subjects but also the European idea of a single certificate, represents a larger step forward than the casual observer can easily recognize. The decision to require from schools and students a twice-a-week course in Theory of Knowledge, not to be examined at the end, successfully compromises the French insistence on philosophy at the close of secondary education with the reluctance of other countries to take much time on such stuff. (This compromise was rescued at the edge of the cliff in the late autumn of 1967, when the members of the philosophy panel, recognizing that courses not sanctioned by examinations tend not to command the best efforts of students, insisted that results in the Theory of Knowledge course be counted for 20% of the mark in the student's social science of history examination. A similar compromise in art proved unacceptable to the art panel, which clamored for a compulsory examination as part of the certificate. Peterson negotiated a substitute arrangement, by which the teacher's grade in these courses could add or subtract one point — out of a possible 120 — to a candidate's total score on the International Baccalaureate.) Finally, the combination of a pass/fail level for the examination itself with the issuance of separate subject certificates for those who fail makes possible the adaptation of the I.B.O. examination to very different national needs and will save future conferences endless hours of debating time.

There remain, however, many problems to be thought through. The schools which started the move toward an International Baccalaureate are all private schools of Anglo-Saxon origin, cherishing an independence from the state and suspicious that all official bodies are at bottom hostile to them.

They are prepared to accept only the barest minimum of governmental inspection, and virtually no governmental supervision. By and large, the American schools in Europe have avoided even the accreditation procedures of the various American voluntary regional school-and-university associations. But it is really not to be expected that the European national authorities will permit their citizens to walk around the national hurdles guarding the door to university unless they have reasonably intimate knowledge of the obstacles the exempted candidates have had to jump. And even the American universities are likely to distrust a call for exemption from Scholastic Aptitude Tests by schools which have not satisfied the requirements of an accrediting body. At the least, I.B.O. will have to grant national authorities the right to inspect — and then to approve or reject — schools which plan to present candidates to universities on the basis of an International Baccalaureate. Indeed, this right of approval of the school is what the French have gained by their conditional acceptance.

All I.B.O. conferences have decided to ignore the possibility of different real standards in different countries, essentially on the grounds that no national system (except the American anarchy) would be willing to admit that its standards for university entrance are lower than those of any other system. Yet it is clearly unfair to hold the American, French or Swedish candidate, going home in the 1970s to a community where perhaps 20% of an age group will enter university, to the standards likely to be demanded in Great Britain or Germany, where national plans call for less than 10% to proceed to university — and neither the British nor the German universities will long accept candidates whose qualifications seem to be clearly below the level of the national entering class. This difficulty might be surmounted by administrative procedure, for there is no intrinsic reason why I.B.O. data should

Conclusion

not be separately submitted to the authorities in different countries, each of which could set its own pass level on the examination.

Most seriously, the intellectual job must still be done. Speed rather than power has been the demand on the participants in the conferences, none of which has lasted long enough to reveal (let alone to reconcile) real differences of cultural or pedagogical approach to subjects. The sort of wrestling with oneself to find reasons of *why* for content and *how* for methodology, which made the American six-week summer science curriculum revision studies so rewarding to their participants, has never emerged at an I.B.O. meeting. Discussions of curricula have been largely trapped in the framework of what the participating teachers are now teaching or might wish to teach; discussions of examination questions have started uniformly from the sort of my-class examination which a teacher wants to give.

With the resources available to I.B.O. thus far, the intellectual aspect of the examination was probably unmanageable; and it can be argued that the failure of the project to explore this ground is a source of hope for the future. For the central fact to emerge from the three years of work toward an international examination is that this is a hard job, which will require considerable efforts from considerable people. Some of these people can indeed be attracted to three-day conferences by personal friendship or generalized goodwill, but they cannot be got to work unless they see the subject as relevant to their own concerns.

Especially in the sciences, where people of very different training work together successfully at many research institutions, first-rate scholars can be attracted to the study of cultural influences on the pedagogy of their disciplines. But someone must place the problem before them, and provide leadership, money, housing and tools, before they can feel confident that the self-questioning which study of this sort requires will lead to deeper understanding rather than to wider malaise.

The reason for traveling, after all, is to learn something about oneself. The quest for an international examination offers this reward at an intellectual and scholarly depth rarely approached by the usual international meeting or multinational project. By widening its focus to include the problem of differing national approaches to education, rather than concentrating so narrowly on the proposed solution of a single examination, I.B.O. might recruit to its service many who would otherwise regard the condition of the international schools as too trivial a subject to warrant their attention. A six-year experiment emphasizing refinements in curricula and examinations would be much more interesting than an experiment biased toward more conventional "educational research."

It is clear that the problems with which I.B.O. has been struggling are real problems. Whatever the weaknesses of the present schema of the examination and of the subject papers, the founders of the Geneva organization raised to the surface a number of questions worth answering. Certainly, something significant must be done for the many adolescents displaced by commercial or political need for their parents' services. Those who will meet this demand in the years to come will owe their success in great measure to the labors of those who created today's first approximation to an international university entrance examination.

INDEX

A

Abitur (examination; Germany), 38, 41, 57, 178, 193
Access to Higher Education (UNESCO), 40
Achievement, levels of: measurement, 190ff., 196ff., 199ff., 203ff., 221
Advanced Placement examinations, 53, 236
Africa: quality of schools in West Africa, 20; school certificates in, 21, 49–50; students from, at foreign universities, 45ff.; national schools with foreign sections, 119–22; diploma standards, 194
Age groups: proportions completing secondary education, 185–86; achievement studies of selected, 199ff.
Allain, Roger, 170
Alliance Française, 54
American College of Paris, 195
American Community School in Athens, 29
"American Family in India, The" (Useem): cited, 19
American International School of Frankfurt, 60, 166–68
American Overseas School of Rome, 159–60

American School of Brussels, 29, 60, 61, 163–65
American School of Guatemala City, 172–74
American School of Japan, Tokyo, 30
American School of Madrid, 24, 60
American School of Mexico City, 61, 171–72
American School of Paris, 160–63, 165–66
American School of Rio de Janeiro, 29, 168–69
American School of Vienna, 60
American University of Beirut, 195
Americanization: of "international" schools, 11
Americans abroad: schools maintained by, 11
Argentina: bilingual studies mandatory, 30; French lycée in Buenos Aires, 150–52
Asia: students from, at foreign universities, 45ff.; diploma standards, 194
Association of Educational and Family Interests of non-Luxembourgian E.C.S.C. Functionaries, 98
Astin, Alexander W., 200
Athens College, 176–77
Atlantic College, Wales, 23, 34,

241

Atlantic College, Wales (*cont.*)
43ff., 62–63, 90–96, 220
Austria: foreign university students in, 48, 50; *see also* Vienna
Autonomous National University of Mexico, 61, 171

B

Baccalauréat (France), 40–41, 188ff.
Baccalaureate, European, *see* European Baccalaureate
Baccalaureate, International, *see* Examination, international
Bagrut (certificate; Israel), 51
Basford, Emory S., 179
Baugh, Richard, 165
Beans, Stanley S., 169
Beeby, Clarence, 112
Beirut: American school at, 30; American University of, 195
Berenson, Irving, 79
Berlin, *see* Französischer Gymnasium; Free University of Berlin; John F. Kennedy School
Bernadotteskolen, Copenhagen, 123–24
Berne, English-Speaking School of, 29
Biases, national: recognition of, 221
Bilingualism, 30ff.; *see also* Language
Boarding schools, proprietary, 8; U. S. private school in Rome, 178–80
Boateng, Eleanor, 121
Bonner, Ruth, 7
Bowles, Frank H.: quoted, 40
Brazil: U. S. schools in, 20, 168–70; French lycée in São Paulo, 148–50; failure rate on *vestibular*, 149
Breier, H., 117
Brewer, Rudolf: quoted, 177–78
Britain: General Certificate of Education, 38; students from former colonies, 49, 50; preparation for university admission, 185; percentage attending university, 186–87; *see also* Overseas schools, British
British School of Montevideo, 146
Brooks, John, 156, 157
Bruce, George, 219, 222; quoted, 184

Brussels: Schola Europaea at, 101, 109; *see also* American School of Brussels
Bucks County, Pennsylvania, 156
Buenos Aires, Argentina: French lycée in, 150–52; University of, 12
Bulgaria: I.B.O. certificate accepted by, 228
Bullard, Donald: quoted, 24, 43
Bureau of Educational and Cultural Affairs (U. S. State Department): cited, 12

C

California: admission to public university, 39
Canada: recognition of U. S. certificates and examinations, 58
Capelle, Jean, 226
Carlsen, Suné: quoted, 48
Carrier, Elisabeth, 122
Carter, Tom, 43ff.
Catholic University, Guatemala, 173
Certificat (Belgium), 41
Children: resistance to internationalization, 34ff.
Children, American: ratio attending foreign schools, 10; achievement of, in foreign schools, 23ff.
Church-related schools, 8
Cohen, Rachel, 125
Cole, Desmond, 86, 227, 231; quoted, 87, 88
Cole-Baker, J. D., 224; quoted, 100
Collège du Léman, Geneva, 73, 127
College Entrance Examination Board, 39
Common Market (European Community): Scholae Europaeae established for, 26, 30, 97ff.; European Baccalaureate treaty signed by members of, 64
Compound schools, 19, 37, 70
Conant, James Bryant, 201
Cook, Russell, 156
Copenhagen, Denmark: international school in, 123
Council of Europe, 48; influence on interchange of students, 194;

Index

Council of Europe (*cont.*)
 comparative studies of achievement, sponsored by, 203ff.
Cour Saint Louis, Stockholm, 122
Crespin, M., 151

D

Davis, Homer W., 176
Denmark: secondary examinations in, 194
Denyer, Arthur, 61, 163; quoted, 60, 164
"Dependent schools," see Military schools, American
DeRosay, Paul, 160
deShalit, Amos: quoted, 37
Desmadryl, Marcel, 106
Deutsche Akademische Austauschdienst, 50
Developing nations, see Underdeveloped countries
Ducret, Bernard: quoted, 50
Dumont, J., 26–27
Dupuy, Paul, 71
Duval, Ted, 124

E

East Africa Examination Council, 50
Ecole Active Bilingue, Paris, 32, 125–26
Ecole Française, New York City, 32
Ecole Internationale de Genève, see International School of Geneva
Ecolint, see International School of Geneva
Eddison, Elizabeth Bole: quoted, 155
Education: need for agreement on definition, 22ff.; concept of international, 69; binational problems exemplified in Französischer Gymnasium, 140–41; binational programs in Uruguay, 146; see also Elementary education; Secondary education
Education and World Affairs (organization), 52, 53
Educational Testing Service, 39

Egypt: students from, in foreign universities, 50
Elementary education: parental attitudes toward, 37
Eliascos, Elias N., 177
England, see Britain
English-Speaking School of Berne, 29
Escola Graduada, São Paulo, 169–70
Euratom: school for staff of, 101
Europe: student mobility in, 48ff.
European Baccalaureate: terms of treaty, 64–65; efforts to devise, 99ff.; structure of examination, 107; examinations for, 208ff.
European Baccalaureate treaty (1957), 64, 101
European Coal and Steel Community: Luxembourg Schola Europaea established for staff of, 97
European Convention (1953), 48
Examination, international: proposals for, 3, 4, 215ff.; feasibility of, 9; U. S. State Department's attitude toward, 12; American participation and support necessary, 14; need for, 63ff.; I.S.A. refusal to support, 100; effect of revised *baccalauréat* on prospects for, 193; proposed ideal, 205ff.; Geneva school curriculum for, 216ff.; 1967 conference on, 226; experimental examination (1967), 228ff.; objective testing, 232; see also European Baccalaureate
Examinations, national: requirements, 10; varying patterns of, 187ff.
Examiners: for I.B.O., 229

F

Ferney-Voltaire, France: government-sponsored school at, 18
First International Baccalaureate Conference (1967), 226
Florida: admission to public university, 39
Forbes, Aleck, 86
Ford Foundation: grant from, 226, 231
Foreign community, resident: schools

Foreign community (cont.)
  sponsored by, 9
"Forgetting curves," 191
Formiga, Francesco, 129
France: Ferney-Voltaire school, 18; foreign university students in, 48; binational treaties on recognition of certificates and examinations, 58, 64; NATO schools closed by, 64; preparation for university admission, 185; percentage attending university, 186; changes in baccalauréat system, 188ff.; see also Overseas schools, French
Franco-Argentinian education treaty, 150
Franco-Brazilian education treaty, 149
Französischer Gymnasium, Berlin, 28, 138-42
Free University of Berlin, 61
French Lycée of London, 54, 57, 142-45
Fuller, Edmund, 179
Furtwängler, Wilhelm, 57

G

Galatasary Lisesi, Istanbul, 60, 69
Gaudin, Augustin: quoted, 143, 189
General Certificate of Education (Britain), 38
Geneva, see International School of Geneva; Lycée des Nations
Georgia: university entrance criteria, 39
German-American cultural exchange program, 168
Germany, see West Germany
Ghana International School, Accra, 76, 119ff.
Gladsaxe Gymnasium, Copenhagen, 32
Goldschmidt, Dietrich, 178
Goodman, Dorothy, 112
Goormaghtigh, John, 224
Gordonstoun school, 91, 92
Government agencies: schools sponsored by, 9
Grading patterns, 191
Grandes Ecoles, 65

Grants, government: for overseas schools, 11-12
Gray, William Scott, 33
Great Britain, see Britain
Greece: foreign university students in, 49
Greek-language elementary schools: in East Africa, 25
Guatemala City: U. S. schools in, 172-74
Gunnell, John, 227

H

Hague, The, see International School of The Hague
Hahn, Kurt, 91
Halls, William D., 6, 186, 203ff., 225, 227; quoted, 193
Hallstein, Walter, 101
Hanson, Harper, 226, 228
Harrari, Maurice: quoted, 53
Harrison, Jack, 166; quoted, 167
Harvard College: admissions policies, 51
Hatinguais, E., 225
Heckscher, August, 4
Hirsch, Etienne, 101
History: teaching of, 4, 216
Hoare, D. J., 23; quoted, 94
Hoffman, G. H., 20
Hoffman, Lionel, 61
Holland, see Netherlands
Holmberg, Harry: quoted, 131
Hopkins, Frank S.: quoted, 12
Houdret, Roger, 145
Houwenstine, Elsie, 6
Husén, Torsten, 186, 199, 205

I

I.E.A., see International Project for the Evaluation of Educational Achievement
I.S.A., see International Schools Association
I.S.E.S., see International Schools Examination Syndicate
Ianuzzelli, Robert: quoted, 159

Index

Ibadan, Nigeria: International School at, 20–21, 26, 120
India: schools sponsored by American and international groups, 19
Intergovernmental agencies: schools sponsored by, 9
International Atomic Energy Agency: efforts to launch a school, 111
International Baccalaureate, *see* Examination, international
International Baccalaureate, The (I.S.E.S.): cited, 230–31
International Baccalaureate Office, 6, 9, 96, 216; conferences on international examination, 218ff.; Council of, 224ff.; limited representation, 233; projections for, 235ff.
International examination, *see* Examination, international
International Project for the Evaluation of Educational Achievement (I.E.A.), 185, 199ff., 202, 204
International School of Geneva (Ecolint), 3, 26, 74; Arab incident, 34; financial problems, 35; emphasis on university admission, 42; in pre-World War II period, 70–72; since World War II, 72–84; curriculum for an International Baccalaureate, 216ff.
International School of Milan, 61, 129–30
International School of The Hague, 19, 112–14
International schools, *see* Schools, multinational
International Schools Association (I.S.A.), Geneva, 74, 86; categories of schools excluded from, 8; refusal to support international examination, 100; international examination proposed at meeting of, 215, 217
International Schools Examination Syndicate (I.S.E.S.), 5, 216; *see also* International Baccalaureate Office
International Schools Foundation, 33
International Schools Services, New York, 156, 157
Internationalizing: resistance of

Internationalizing (*cont.*)
children to, 34ff.
Iran: French nationals not admitted to French-financed schools in, 19; students from, in foreign universities, 50
Istanbul, *see* Galatasary Lisesi
Italy: binational treaties on recognition of certificates and examinations, 58

J

Japan, American School of, 30
Johannot, Jean, 128
John F. Kennedy School, Berlin, 61, 154, 177–78
"Junior year abroad" program, 53

K

Kabul: American school at, 30
Kahn, Brian, 88
Keynes, John Maynard, 220
Knight, Michael: quoted, 76
Korea: students from, in foreign universities, 50
Krouse, Stanley W., Jr., 170

L

Lagos: American school in, 34
Lamco (company), 130
Language: ability of children to learn new, 23; study of local, in American overseas schools, 29ff.; as determining factor in choice of foreign university, 47; common-language areas, and university admission, 58ff.; in Common Market schools, 65, 102; increasing influence of English, 72; French and English in overseas schools, 177; teaching of, 221ff.
Latin America: regional agreements on university admission, 58; U.S. schools in, 61, 168, 171–74; diploma standards in, 194
Lauwerys, Joseph, 112

Leach, Robert, 7, 83, 216, 217; quoted, 76
Lebanon: *baccalauréat* of, accepted by France, 50
Legrand, Albert: quoted, 20
Lejeune, René, 150; quoted, 148–49
LeRosey, Geneva, 127–29
Liberia: Yekepa school, 26, 130–31
Lincoln American School, Buenos Aires, 12, 30, 34, 62, 69, 174–76
Literature, teaching of: suggested curriculum, 4; at Scholae Europaeae, 106–07
London: lycée in, 54, 57, 142–45; University of, 49
Lumumba University, Moscow, 48
Luxembourg: Schola Europaea in, 97ff., 109–10
Lycée Chateaubriand, Rome, 135–38
Lycée des Nations, Geneva, 73
Lycée Français de Montevideo, 145–48
Lycée Henri IV, Paris, 32
Lycée of Buenos Aires, 150–52
Lycée Pasteur, São Paulo, 148–50
Lycées d'outre-mer, see Overseas schools, French

M

MacVean, Robert, 172
Maddison, Angus, 45
Madrid, *see* American School of Madrid
Mannino, Ernest N.: quoted, 174
Manuel, Janine, 125; quoted, 126
Martin, Georges-Henri, 3
Martin, Nan: quoted, 78
Massachusetts Institute of Technology, 196
Mathematics: teaching of, 4, 223
Matura (certificate; Austria), 57
Maturité (certificate; Switzerland), 51, 57
Maurette, Thérèse, 71
Mayan School, Guatemala City, 173–74
Mayer, René, 99
McKee, Douglas, 160
McPherson, Harry C., Jr., 12

Merchant Taylors' school, London, 32
Metropolitan countries: acceptance of university students from former colonies, 49ff.; attitudes of former colonies toward, 232
Mexico: U.S. schools in, 61, 171–72; *see also* Autonomous National University of Mexico
Meyer, Jean: quoted, 77
Milan, *see* International School of Milan
Military schools, American, 7, 23ff.
Mission schools, 19, 69
Mittleman, Naum, 12, 174
Mobility of population: educational problems engendered by, 17ff.
Monnet, Jean, 98
Montevideo: British school at, 146; lycée at, 145–48
Moran, Brother: quoted, 62
Morgan, Anthony, 144; quoted, 41–42
Morot-Sir, Edouard: quoted, 19
Multinational schools, *see* Schools, multinational

N

NATO schools: in France, 26, 64
Nawar, Asmy, 6
Nelson, David, 127
Netherlands: quality of education, 19; foreign university students in, 47
"New Links" (pamphlet), 156; cited, 33
New York City, *see* Ecole Française; United Nations International School
New York State: admission to public university, 39
Nicolaus Cusanus Gymnasium, Bad Godesberg, 114, 116–17
Nido de Aguilas, Santiago de Chile, 171
Nigeria: International School of Ibadan, 20–21, 26, 120
Nimmons, Chester, 89
Non-military schools, *see* Overseas schools; Schools, multinational
Norway: foreign university students in, 49

Index

O

Office du Baccalauréat (France), 38, 40
Office of Overseas Schools (U.S. State Department): guidelines for grants to schools, 11, 158
Office of U.S. Programs and Services (U.S. State Department): attitude toward International Baccalaureate project, 12
Ollivera, Denise, 144
Ostergaard, Ulf, 86, 123
"Outward Bound," 91, 92, 94
Overseas schools: university admission pressure in, 41
Overseas schools, American: advantages of internationalizing, 13; local language study, 29ff.; teaching methods, 33; students prepared only for U.S. examinations, 62; geographical spread, 154; lack of professionalism, 155; financial problems, 157ff.; as an organism of environment, 159
Overseas schools, British, 153–54
Overseas schools, French, 14, 19, 50, 133–52; budget for, 133; recruitment and assignment of staffs, 134–35; varying patterns of, 135ff.
Oxford University: Rhodes Scholars at, 49
Oxford University, Department of Education, 6, 225, 231

P

Panchaud, G., 224, 225
Panel on Educational Research and Development, 4
Paris, see American School of Paris; Ecole Active Bilingue; Lycée Henri IV
Parsons, Gordon: quoted, 60
Patterson, John C., 178–80
Peterson, A. D. C., 6, 195, 225, 226, 227, 229, 237
Petri, Bengt, 186
Pezet, Maurice, 87
Phillips, Donald, 165
Pidgeon, D. A., 205
Pierce College, Athens, 177
Pilotti, Massimo, 98
Poirel, Nancy, 79
Poland: emphasis on bilingual education, 31
Poppinga, Bein: quoted, 106, 107
Postlethwaite, T. Nelson, 205; quoted, 206, 207
Private schools, see Boarding schools, proprietary; Church-related schools; Compound schools; Schools, multinational
Proposals to Establish an International School in Washington: Feasibility Study, 111, 112
Prueba de aptitud académica (examination; Chile), 187
Public Law 480, 158

Q

Quito, Ecuador: U.S. schools in, 174

R

Rasquin, Michel, 98
Red Cross, 70
Renaud, Gérard, 229; quoted, 219
Rio de Janeiro, see American School of Rio de Janeiro
Robert College, Istanbul, 60
Rockefeller, John D., Jr., 71
Rocquet, Alfred, 81
Rome, see American Overseas School of Rome; Lycée Chateaubriand; St. Stephen's School
Rossano, Claire, 144
Rourke, Robert E. K., 178, 180, 219
Russia: emphasis on bilingual education, 31; foreign university students in, 48

S

Saint-Germain-en-Laye: NATO lycée at, 26, 117–19
Santiago de Chile: French lycée at,

Santiago de Chile (*cont.*)
14; U. N. regional center at, 18; U.S. school in, 171

São Paulo: lycée in, 35, 148–50; *see also* Escola Graduada

Scandinavia: schools for international community, 122ff.

Schaller, Victor: quoted, 42

Scherer, E.: quoted, 27

Schneider, Horst, 139; quoted, 141

Scholae Europaeae, 26, 30, 31; claims made by, 33; language in, 65, 102; early development, 97ff.; in Luxembourg, 97ff., 109–10; curriculum, 102ff., 191; in Varese, 103, 105, 106, 108; success in terms of university admissions, 105; as models for international schools, 111; international examination at, 208ff.; *see also* European Baccalaureate

Scholastic Aptitude Test, 40, 187, 236

Schools: sponsored by resident foreign community and by government agencies, 9; *see also* Boarding schools, proprietary; Church-related schools; Compound schools; Overseas schools

Schools, multinational, 7, 10, 11; inevitability of, 25; centrifugal forces, 35; cultural diffusion possible in, 36; university admission pressure in, 41, 42; need for single certificate, 63ff.; prototypes, 74, 111; foreign students in schools primarily for local residents, 114ff.; *see also* Scholae Europaeae

Schools, Society and Progress in France (Halls), 193

Science: teaching of, 13–14, 87, 196–97, 221

Scotland: preparation for university admission, 185

Secondary education: diversity in national examinations, 10; definitions of acceptability, 18; denationalization as result of foreign, 37; examinations for validation of, 38; binational treaties on recognition of

Secondary education (*cont.*)
certificates, 58ff.; evaluation of, by universities, 183–84; proportions of varying age groups completing, 185–86; French reforms in, 192, 193; in U.S. compared with European, 194ff.

Sellars, Jack, 229

Sèvres, France: experimental lycée at, 115

Shirar, Robert: quoted, 60

Siotis, Jean, 6, 225

Sly, John, 6, 158

Smith-Mundt Act (1948), 158

Snell, David S., 120; quoted, 52

South America, *see* Latin America

Spaak, Paul-Henri, 98

Spain: *bachillerato* of Latin American countries accepted by, 50

Specialization: in university studies, 196; in last years of secondary school, 222

St. Stephen's School, Rome, 178–80

Standing Conference of Culture Ministries (Germany), 51

Stiftelsen Viggbyholmskolan, 123

Stoyle, P. B., 146

Studentexamen (certificate; Sweden), 61

Students: at foreign universities, 45ff.

Sweden: foreign university students in, 47; schools for international community, 122ff.; percentage attending university, 186–87; changes in examination system, 190

Sweetser, Arthur, 156; quoted, 70, 71–72

Switzerland: acceptance of students from developing nations in universities of, 50; proprietary "international" schools, 126ff.

Syllabi, 4, 63, 83, 87, 207, 216, 229, 232

"Syndicates" (Britain), 38

T

Taiwan: students from, in foreign universities, 50

Index

Tallon, G.: quoted, 134, 135
Taylor, Andrew, 120
Teheran: American school at, 30
Tests, cross-cultural, 203, 212
Tests, objective, 232
Thévenin, André, 146; quoted, 147
Thomas, Philip, 82–83
Thought patterns: relationship to verbal formulations, 31
Tokyo school, see American School of Japan
Tourism, 32
Treaties, binational, 58ff., 64
Turkey: French nationals not admitted to French-financed schools in, 19
Twentieth Century Fund: grant from, 5, 218, 231
Tyler committee: cited, 45, 52

U

Underdeveloped countries: problem of international schools, 18–19; foreign schooling for children of, 32; investment in foreign education, 46; attitudes toward foreign education for nationals, 231–32
UNIS, see United Nations International School, New York City
United Nations International School, New York City, 26, 30, 84–90, 227; Educational Policies Committee, cited, 36
United States: university admission systems, 39, 185; foreign university students in, 48, 50; recognition of Canadian certificates and examinations, 58; percentage attending university, 186–87; secondary education in, compared with European, 194ff.; see also Overseas schools, American
United States, Department of State: attitude toward International Baccalaureate project, 11–12
Universities: in Asia, 7; entrance examinations, 38ff., 184ff.; admissions problems, 41, 45ff., 185, 238; inter-
Universities (cont.)
university student transfers in Europe, 49; admission of foreign students in Germany, 50; admission policies of American, 51ff.; acceptance of American students by foreign, 53; admission of nationals with foreign secondary schooling, 56ff.
University of Buenos Aires Faculty of Exact Sciences, 12
University of Ibadan, Nigeria: International School, 20–21, 26, 120
University of London, 49
University of Milan, 61
University of Sofia: I.B.O. certificate accepted for entrance, 228
University of the Americas, 172
Uruguay: French lycée in, 145–46
U.S.S.R., see Russia
Useem, Ruth Hill: quoted, 19, 43

V

Vaizey, John, 229
Valentine, Robert: quoted, 236
van der Mensbrugghe, Jean: quoted, 37, 38
Van Der Valk, Jan, 62, 112–14; quoted, 19, 28
van Houtte, Albert, 97ff., 112, 215, 219
van Smevoorde, E., 222
Varese, Italy: Schola Europaea in, 103, 105, 106, 108
Verbal formulations: relationship to thought patterns, 31
Vestibular (examination; Brazil), 149
Vienna: French lycée and "international" school at, 26, 34; American school at, 60
Voss, Karl: quoted, 101

W

Wallach, Eugene, 7
Weber, Mirian, 81
West Africa: quality of schools in, 20

West African Examinations Council, 50
West African School Certificate, 21
West Germany: foreign university students in, 48; control of education vested in states, 50; acceptance of students from developing nations in universities of, 50; preparation for university admission, 185; percentage attending university, 186–87; secondary examinations in, 193ff.

Y

Yekepa (Liberia) school, 26, 130–31